MINNESOTA
WILD

Printed in Hong Kong.

89 90 91 92 93 8 7 6 5 4

ISBN 0-89658-029-6

Published by Voyageur Press, Inc.
P.O. Box 338
123 North Second Street
Stillwater, MN 55082 U.S.A.
In Minn 612-430-2210
Toll Free 800-888-9653

Voyageur Press books are also available at discounts in bulk quantities for premium or sales-promotion use. For details contact the Marketing Manager. Please write or call for our free catalog of natural history publications.

MINNESOTA WILD

Text and Photographs
by Les Blacklock
and Craig Blacklock

Voyageur Press

In memory of our friend Sig Olson, whose voice will
forever resonate among the echoes of the voyageurs —

CONTENTS

Lichen-draped white spruce, Susie Island

MINNESOTA WILD

Les

All across northern Minnesota, from Red Lake to Pigeon Point, are bogs and fens — carpets of wet land that support ancient, stunted trees, flowering shrubs, and a rich treasure of the most precious of flowers, the orchids. In vegetation, appearance, and climate, this could be the south edge of the arctic.

Surrounding these intriguing but little known bogs are boreal forests of pine, cedar, spruce, and balsam — the north woods. To the west the forests become aspen and aspen parkland. They blend with, and finally give way to, a lush garden of prairie grasses and flowers. This is the eastern edge of the tall-grass prairie.

South of the boreal forest is mixed timber, becoming the classic maple-basswood forest in The Big Woods and a rich mixture of hardwoods in the bluff country of the Mississippi River and its tributaries in the southeast.

Like a scattering of sapphires on green velvet, thousands of lakes lie in a strewn pattern across the state. A number of these lakes are too big to see across, and yet they are like ponds next to the greatest of the world's lakes, Superior. Minnesota's North Shore is 150 miles of Precambrian cliffs, broad rock slopes, and sweeping curves of beaches; in appearance a rugged ocean coast, but the water is sweet and clean.

Across this broad and fascinating land are marshes, ponds, swamps, streams, rivers, meadows, sand dunes, goat prairies, islands — habitats in unlimited variety and size, from minute lichen gardens to the largest stands of virgin eastern white pine in the nation.

It is nature's way that for every variation in habitat, every niche, there is a creature or plant to fill that niche. In Minnesota that means we enjoy the presence of an extraordinary variety of plants and animals.

And to add even more diversity to the landscape, four dramatically different seasons change not only the broad scene from chartreuse to green to gold to white, but bring a look-now-or-you'll-miss-it succession of flowers and birds that make just being in one place a constant adventure.

It is pure luck (and our good fortune) that this dramatic meeting of geographic differences from north, south, east, and west takes place in Minnesota, and that bedrock at the surface, extensive wetlands, and rocky soil have kept many wild places from being developed.

Minnesota Wild is the natural beauty of our state; it is what we see, hear, and feel as we paddle the Boundary Waters, hike the woodland trails, look across whole mountains of fall color in the Sawtooth Range, watch skeins of waterfowl and hear their haunting calls over the prairie. It is the *ka-whump* of powerful surf on the North Shore, acres of pink laurel in a northern bog, tom turkeys gobbling on the wooded slopes above the Whitewater, fragrant water lilies floating on a beaver pond.

It is that soft-aired, golden, seventy-degree day in Indian summer when you wish the clock could stop for just a few hours.

It is Minnesota at her natural best, and she is beautiful.

WILD SHORES

Les

Lakes

Ogishkemuncie, Winnibigoshish, Minnetonka, Pepin, Carlos, Shetek, Katrina. Most Minnesotans will recognize at least some of these names of Minnesota lakes. If you know the lakes, each name conjures an image which is very different from the others. Ogish is granite anchored, glacier scoured, island studded; Big Winnie is huge, rush shored, pine bordered; Minnetonka is sprawling, many bayed, high banked, maple hemmed; Pepin is long, deep set, bluff guarded.

I have but *touched* four lakes, yet the impossibility of describing a few as representative of Minnesota's lakes is obvious. To write about Leech and say that Cass and Winnie and Mille Lacs are more of the same would not only be inaccurate, it would be unfair.

Twelve thousand of almost anything could be boring. But *not* 12,000 lakes! Every lake I've met has been a joy. To stand on the edge of a lake of any size is to stand on the edge of wildness. I have watched black-crowned night herons fish in Minneapolis's Lake Harriet, I've seen a moose slip ghostlike into fog-dimmed cattails on the edge of Mud Lake at Lake Agassiz National Wildlife Refuge, and I've watched a midsummer sunrise over Kabetogama from high on the rock outcrops in Voyageurs National Park.

There are lots of Round Lakes, Long Lakes, and Mud Lakes in Minnesota. And more than a few numbered lakes. Not every lake namer was a poet. But several lakes are poets: Pope, Keats, Shelley, and Homer. And one is called Poet Lake. It seems that the namers, once they got on a theme, had an easy time naming the next few lakes, like Cucumber, Turnip, Parsnip, Bean, Tomato, Carrot, Potato, and Celery.

Many lake names have a colorful connection with the past. They say that Devil Track Lake got its name from the mystifying trail in the snow of a peg-legged man crossing the lake.

The Indian names sound as if they belong. At least they relate to the lakes better than a number or the name of a nonnative vegetable: Gabimichigami, Saganaga, Kawishiwi, Tuscarora, Kitchi.

But even if a lake is named Lake 16 or Stooey-Dooey, it doesn't change the looks of that lake, nor do any wild visitors stay away because of the name. I have canoed on Stooey-Dooey in summer and snowshoed its boreal forest shores in winter. It's a lovely lake. In a consulting naturalist study of the area, I suggested it be renamed Sig Olson Lake. It is quiet. And handsome. And a pleasure to be with. Like Sig.

Bald eagle bringing fish to young, Chippewa National Forest

I have always lived with lakes. My father fly-fished the rapids that slurp over and between the stones at the outlet of Moose Lake. And so did I. We often trolled in an old wooden rowboat for late-feeding walleyes on Sturgeon Lake until midnight. There would be long periods without a word being spoken, yet I remember those quiet hours as some of the best we spent together. Our whole world was there in that path of moonlight. The lonesome call of the loon or the whishing wings of bluebills were the only sounds other than the lap of water on the boat and the repeated small splashes of the oars.

If we went too long without a strike, there'd be a few whispered words, a reeling in of lines, a brief period of searching for more promising lures with a weak flashlight, then quiet again. Sometimes hooking a weed would mean retrieving the lure for a check. Looking against the moon's path of sparkles we could see even minute bits of weed in silhouette, pick them off, and go back to trolling.

The submerged bar we fished was quite far from shore, but by lining up familiar pine trees in two directions, we crossed that bar several times during the night of fishing, and each time we'd expect a strike.

Some of our most challenging fishing was night fishing for largemouth bass in Section Eleven Lake. Casting favorite plugs like the wiggly Teas Oreno toward a black mass that was shore was tricky. If there was no splash, the plug landed on shore, and we jerked high and hard to get the lure off the land, hoping it wasn't hooked on anything. The object was to cast the plug within a couple of yards of shore, hoping that a big bass waiting there for a frog to jump in would strike at it. We'd wind in the lure a few feet at a time, then let it rest on the water, teasing a bass to strike. We caught lots of lily pads, quite a few bulrushes, and once in a while a nice bass.

The size of a lake, its depth, the kind of bottom it has, the vegetation in it, and the flow through it have much to do with what kind of a lake it is. But the *shore* determines what a lake is like to the beholder.

The sand beaches with pine shores in the Brainerd-Bemidji country are quite different from the hardwood-bordered beaches around Alexandria and Detroit Lakes. In contrast to these are the shallow wild-rice-filled lakes of north central Minnesota and the western prairie sloughs, which might be the most exciting places in the state for birders. I've been happily stunned by the roar of wings of thousands of northern diving ducks in fall migration at the Rice Lake National Wildlife Refuge, and I've been equally moved by a dozen huge white pelicans, with their nine-foot wingspan, gliding in to a surfboard-type landing at Salt Lake near Madison in April.

Sometimes I have the feeling that almost all of the wild shores will soon be gone. City people commute great distances to live by a lake. Many small town families have moved out to surrounding lakes. Hundreds of lakes are already encircled by cabins and country homes. So much of the original prairie was wet — in sloughs, marshes, and shallow lakes — that drainage became a way of life to make more cropland. According to Department of Natural Resources (DNR) figures, thirteen million acres were drained.

On the positive side, the DNR Save-the-Wetlands Program and the United States Fish and Wildlife Service Acquisition Program have acquired 575,000 acres of sloughs and marshes, slowing run-off to ease downstream flooding, keeping water tables high to provide adequate moisture for croplands, and providing wildlife habitat. Those wetlands belong to all of us. And so do most of the lakes in the Boundary Waters Canoe Area Wilderness (BWCAW), Superior and Chippewa national forests, fifty-five state forests, plus county forests, state parks, game refuges, park reserves, and nature centers. These add up to a lot of wild shores!

Rivers and Streams

I suppose that sky divers, when they step from a plane, are about as committed as anyone can be. They are quite certain what they will be doing the next couple of minutes.

Canoeists make a similar commitment. Once they are being sucked into the top of a rapids it's a little late to change their minds.

Craig and I committed ourselves to about fifty rapids on a 130-mile stretch of the Big Fork River that flows north to the Rainy River on the Ontario border. I paddled bow so I could photograph from the canoe and take notes as we went along. What follows is a selection from my notes.

July 6: We have just arrived from home, set up camp, and are out for an evening paddle to get acquainted with the Big Fork. Above the nettles and grasses on the riverbank, a pair of monarch butterflies are performing an aerial courtship dance that makes us wonder how any creatures can have that much energy. The backdrop of green ash and silver maples looks like any floodplain forest in southern Minnesota, not at all what we expected to find up here in the north woods.

Yellow-crowned night heron! No doubt about it. My first ever. It stood tall and stared from beneath the canopy of a great silver maple. His gray breast and unique head pattern gave double proof that this handsome bird is really up here, way north of where it is supposed to be.

July 7: Push-off 6:24 A.M. Great blue heron lifts off from foggy cattails. Hen wood duck flies, squealing; ducklings scuttle across to taller cover. Woodpecker very loud and jazz-rhythmic, breaks the morning quiet . . . Great horned owl drops in a swooping, inverted arch to a tree farther downstream. Two young spotted sandpipers flit past and light on a gray log at river's edge . . . White-breasted nuthatches and chickadees calling. Flicker announces itself from top of dead elm. Morning light turns everything gold. Bullfrog clucking back in a bay. Blue common skullcaps and purple swamp milkweed make a nice color combination with green sedges, cattails, and river bulrushes, all brushed with wisps of morning fog.

Kingfishers dive for minnows ahead of us . . . Slow current doesn't give much warning of large boulders just under the surface. Long streamers of underwater plants undulate like Hawaiian skirts . . . Water smartweed leaves cover the river's surface . . . Tall balsams and white spruce on higher slopes. Worn places on riverbanks show where beavers have dragged aspen logs to the river.

A muskrat swam across from wild rice bed to a screen of ash roots on the riverbank, dragging vegetation behind it. We followed to within two feet of the roots. We could hear it chewing and chirping, sounding as if it enjoyed its salad . . . Cedar waxwings and cliff swallows catching insects over the river; common bittern flew past us heading upstream.

We've set up camp in a grove of virgin white cedars. After many miles of floodplain forest, it's nice to find these north-woods friends. I'm sitting with my back to one of the big trees; the quiet river flows slowly just below me. Upstream seven great moss-covered cedars lean gracefully over the water, filtering the evening sun.

July 8: Two canoes in a three-canoe group ahead of us just swamped. One of the canoes is flat against a large rock with the open top upstream, scooping in the water — about as stuck as you can get and a good way to fold a canoe . . . It took Craig and five others to free the canoe. Craig sized up the rapids and has assured me we can run it. Here we go! . . . Smooth as silk. I'm a little wet from the spray but that feels good on this hot day.

We are at Little American Falls. Understated signs upstream said, "Caution, Rapids." It is actually a roaring waterfall.

July 9: Both of us felt sore muscles this morning, but a cup of coffee and a superb north-woods breakfast started the day right. Last night Craig cast into the eddies below the falls and caught a small northern pike just at dusk. He filleted it on a paddle blade while I held a flashlight. We both slapped ourselves often, and mosquitoes sometimes. This morning Craig buttered and salt-and-peppered the fillets, wrapped them in foil, and buried them in a bed of coals. In a few minutes the steaming packets of flaky white meat were opened and eaten with gusto.

Water striders make tiny flashes evenly spaced on the dark green reflections ahead, then scoot in all directions when we get close . . . Broad-winged hawk just dropped from overhead branch and looped up to an ash across the river. Long fronds of black ash and ostrich ferns add junglelike touch to the forest.

Got a close look at a mink on a floating log before it zipped to shore and up a steep bank . . . Beaver surfaced just ten feet from the canoe . . . A beautiful yearling black bear cub ran off into thick shrubs before I could get a picture . . . An osprey circled over us in its search for fish; then a male scarlet tanager, the brightest red possible, flew by.

We saw a doe downstream eating from the crown of a fallen ash tree, and Craig eased us along the shaded bank toward her. She saw us but didn't leap away until we were almost up to her.

Our canoe map says we've paddled 38½ miles today to our camp at Johnson's Landing. While we were making camp, a weasel, summer brown, stood tall in the woodpile for an instant to inspect me. We're having supper, and guess who's poking around camp? A *skunk*, with no fear of us whatsoever. We holler, jump, slap and roar, but all she does is sniff and come closer. She just went into the tent, explored, and came out again. What she's after is in our hands — our food.

Mother skunk disappeared for a few minutes and is now back with her baby, a cute miniature of her, and both are cavorting all over camp, wherever they wish to go.

I zipped up the screen on the tent door and now

Mille Lacs Lake

the mother is bumping into the screen again and again, trying to find the opening, falling all over herself like a circus clown.

July 11: Sometime in the middle of last night the back end of our tent caved in on top of us. Instinctively I pushed up on the canvas and realized I was holding up a skunk. Craig woke up shouting at what he thought was a bear. I shushed him, hoping we wouldn't trigger our well-armed visitor, and waited for her next move. She finally climbed down and hopped around to the front of the tent. In the bright moonlight we could see her clearly as she charged the netting time after time, trying to get in. Now Craig was trying to keep *me* quiet. Fortunately she left us with only a broken tent pole, which we had improvised in the first place from a not-too-sturdy piece of wood we found at the campsite. We usually string the tent between trees, but there were no convenient ones at the landing.

July 12: After our eventful night, a deer blew a "good morning" to us from nearby as we pushed off . . . Mallards, common and hooded mergansers occasionally fly up ahead of us . . . River has broadened to about two hundred feet. High hills on both sides now; we've left the floodplain forests.

July 13: Below Gowdy campsite there are old homestead clearings here and there. Big cedars and pines have bark battered off by spring ice floes as high as fifteen feet above the river level. We stopped on a sand-gravel bar for a rest and lunch. Tracks of deer, beaver, bobcat, skunk, and raccoon . . . We made it to our destination at Lindford as rolling black clouds, spitting lightning, were ready to burst like a paper bag full of water. Our tent was set up and everything inside when the storm hit.

(In our paddle down the Big Fork, Craig and I used one of forty river canoe maps available free from the Minnesota Department of Natural Resources.)

Minnesota's 25,000 miles of rivers and streams — enough to circle the globe at the equator — leave the state via four major watersheds. Lake Superior drainage reaches the Atlantic Ocean through the Great Lakes. The Red River of the North and the Rainy River send Minnesota water on its way to Hudson Bay. The southwest corner of the state is part of the Missouri watershed, and the great Mississippi drains the rest of the state.

From ice-cold springs and air-clear trout streams in the north and southeast, to the broad floodplain wilderness of the Mississippi bottoms, from the family-outing Crow River to the rolling, skill-testing Kettle, Minnesota's moving water has something for everyone.

I've waded and paddled down the Stump River and flushed out seven moose in one day, and I watched in awe one April day as only dangling cables remained of the old swinging bridge in Jay Cooke State Park, destroyed by the force of the raging St. Louis River. On another spring day our family, with friends, paddled down the sparkling Rum — warm sun, spring flowers, frogs and birds — delightful.

The St. Croix River, shared along much of its length with neighboring Wisconsin, is one of the nicest things to happen between two states. One of its most spectacular places is the Dalles of the St. Croix at Taylors Falls. Hundred-foot, vertical-walled rock cliffs confine the churning river to its twisting channel. White pines crown the cliffs and outcrops.

It is obvious that a much larger river carved the St. Croix Valley. Geologists tell us that Glacial Lake Duluth, formed when the big glaciers started to melt, overflowed moraines and poured a huge torrent southward to the St. Croix. The racing flood carried glacial debris with it, and stones bouncing along the bottom dropped into holes or fissures of the lava rock and spun in whirlpools, wearing circular, deep potholes, or kettles, up to a dozen feet across and sixty or more feet deep.

Farther upstream, Wild River State Park and St. Croix State Park are not as spectacular as the Dalles, but are more remote. Early one spring morning at Wild River, I watched five deer cross a floodplain meadow, heading for the river, far from cover. They were being very brash and they knew it, so they were doubly cautious. Every step was studied, each hoof held up for a few seconds, then carefully and soundlessly placed. Ears twisted this way and that. Heads turned, eyes stared. Like kids playing follow-the-leader, they dared to do it, but it was derring-do all the way.

There is a small beach of the finest sand at the base of a pine-covered bank at St. Croix State Park east of Hinckley. I was there at dawn, but something had been there ahead of me. The track of a single deer, cleanly printed where the sand was damp, marked its maker's passing. I avoided walking on the beach; my boot print would have been an intrusion.

When I was young, few people hiked in wild places except during hunting seasons, so I often had

Little American Falls, Big Fork River

White cedars overhanging the Big Fork River

Smartweed floating on the surface of the Big Fork River

Dalles of the St. Croix, Interstate State Park

Pothole, Dalles of the St. Croix

St. Croix River, St. Croix State Park

the whole valley of the Moose Horn River downstream from our town to myself. This combination of wildness and privacy resulted in some experiences that are indelible in my memory.

In early spring, when surrounding lakes were still frozen, migrating waterfowl concentrated on the open river, and I was there — before breakfast, after school, all day on weekends; I didn't want to miss any part of it.

One warm Saturday morning there were just patches of slushy snow left; rivulets and pools were everywhere. I had to jump across wet places to keep from going in over my well-oiled leather boots. Finding a partly concealed dry place to sit at river's edge, I sat with my knees drawn up under my chin and watched, stock-still. A great blue heron sailed in to fish near the only island on that part of the river. Lesser scaups, goldeneyes, and hooded mergansers flew over, circled, and landed on various parts of the broad, slow, shallow river. To a twelve-year-old kid this was the ultimate of what life had to offer; it couldn't get any better than this.

I was suddenly aware of something big and close, upriver, coming from my left. I didn't blink. Five feet from shore a loon was swimming my way, and if it didn't turn or dive it was going to be five feet from me! I held my breath. The great black-and-white bird came on silently, smoothly, unswervingly. The ruby-red eyes always stare, but at that closest instant — the nearest I would ever be to a wild loon — that right eye was staring at *me*.

When it was straight out from me it started to sink. Continuing past me at the same slow, steady rate, it simply sank deeper and deeper, like a submarine, until only its head showed, kept on sinking, and disappeared.

My trail from home in town to the wild valley led across a railroad trestle over the river. From that vantage point I had watched the spectacular aerial dance of the woodcock silhouetted against colorful spring sunsets. But I had never had a close-up look at the bird. They are camouflaged to the point of invisibility until they fly.

But one day, stalking slowly through an alder thicket, I saw one before it saw me. The plump bird poked its long bill straight down into the mud floor again and again, and every once in a while brought up a squirming earthworm. I didn't move, and the timberdoodle came to within a few feet of me. I've since learned that it can bend just the tip of its bill to grasp the worm underground and that it eats up to half its weight in worms each day.

The shores of the Moose Horn were alive with wildlife — beavers, herons, muskrats, deer, ruffed grouse. Creatures of both forest and water were there. Sometimes I would inch on my belly to within a few feet of hooded mergansers, then suddenly stand up in full sight of the handsome birds. Their great crests would rise to full fan and they'd swim away, looking back at me in disbelief before taking off. I didn't have that close-up view for long, but what an exciting few seconds!

There's a little stream that tumbles down through the forest to the Moose Horn. At one point it cascades between and over large flat boulders. More often than not, this is where I'd take my paper bag out of my pack and eat my lunch. Life was good.

Marsh marigolds, Portage Brook, Superior National Forest

THE MARSH DANCERS

Craig

A redwing flashed his crimson epaulets, tilting this way and that as he called out atop a swaying cattail. The breeding season had brought a new vitality into the flooded brown marsh, and with it, the exuberant music of spring.

In the distance a wild, screeching *cree-cree! cree-cree!* stabbed through all the other voices. It was the call of a western grebe. Other grebes soon joined in the calling, and I prepared for a morning among the marsh dancers.

I had come to a marsh on the floodplain of the Minnesota River just below its source at Big Stone Lake. Behind me were prairie-covered bluffs and a thin border of cottonwoods and willows. Before me lay the marsh — a wide expanse of open water and emergent vegetation bustling with life.

I put on my chest-high waders, closed a floating portable blind over myself, and sloshed into the three and a half feet of water. Bubbles of swamp gas, methane, escaped from the muck with each of my steps. The gas is a product of decay, a clue to what is happening and how marshes are formed.

Unlike bog vegetation, which grows in a floating mat out over lakes, marsh plants are rooted in the muddy bottoms of shallow shores. As generations of plants and animals die, their matter is broken down by bacteria and fungi, adding to the muck on the bottom. This muck, together with debris washed in from run-off, gradually fills in lakes and ponds, a process known as eutrification. As the water gets shallower the deep-water plants of lakes and ponds give way to marsh vegetation such as arrowhead and cattails. These may later be replaced by sedges and, finally, by woody plants, by which time only a moist meadow will mark what was once an open body of water.

Suddenly I felt a heavy "something" thrashing against my legs. Looking down in the shadow of my blind, I saw a giant carp gliding away. I soon realized I was sharing the water with thousands of these rough fish. Apparently spawning, they flopped about among the cattails and constantly bumped my legs as I made my way through the marsh.

I waded from a large area of open water into a maze of small channels surrounded by cattails. A pair of ruddy ducks floated by. With his tail fanned turkey-style, the drake performed comical head bobs and "rubber duck" squeaks designed to attract his mate — appropriate antics from a little round duck with a permanent blue smile.

Grebes were calling all around me, but none were yet visible. Then two pairs of the swanlike birds came into view from the open water, their

Yellow-headed blackbird

Red-winged blackbird

striking black-and-white plumage and fiery red eyes reflecting in the still water. Stiletto bills opened in calls that stung with their vibrancy. The birds that had been concealed in the marsh around me glided out to meet the newcomers, and the opening now held more than a dozen.

Tension built while the grebes stretched their heads back over their bodies in a preening show, white breasts glistening as they crisscrossed the water. Two birds swam rapidly toward each other, low in the water with necks out and dark crests spread, beaks cutting through the surface. Then they stopped abruptly, facing off only inches apart.

Five quick turns of their heads and the wrought-up energy exploded. They rose upright on churning feet, turning in mirrored unison. Side-by-side, with arched necks high and beaks forward, they "rushed," running erect over the surface of the water with wings held back, for perhaps twenty feet before ending their dance in a dive. This excitement sparked others into dancing, and reflections were transformed into glittering sparkles.

I eased along an edge of the cattails and came upon a number of grebes' nests. Each floating platform of woven vegetation had been anchored to a cattail clump, allowing the nests to adjust to changing water levels and to be safe from shore-bound predators. A bird that had already begun setting stood up and carefully turned four light tan eggs.

Both parents incubate the eggs and take equal responsibility in caring for the young. When the young are hatched, they will ride a great deal of the time on their parents' backs, cradled in the adults' wings.

I was wading back to my camp when ahead of me an intimate and touching display unfolded — the grebes' "wedding dance."

A pair had just surfaced from a dive, bits of weeds in their bills. Barely stirring the surface, they treaded water, lifting half of their upright bodies out of the water. Like two serpents charming each other, they wove their heads and necks back and forth while slowly circling around. Settling back into the water, they disappeared into the cattails.

By summer the marsh was overflowing with new life. Tadpoles and fish fry swam about in the shallows; newborn turtles scrambled from their earthen birthplaces down to the relative safety of the water. Dozens of ducklings and goslings trailed their mothers among the emergent plants. But

nowhere were the young more conspicuous than at the heron rookery.

In mid-July I paddled out to the island of dead, nest-festooned trees and was greeted with the raucous calling of cormorants, herons, and egrets.

The nesting spots had been divided among the birds, with the safest locations being taken by the largest. Great blue herons occupied the highest nests in the center of the island. Below them were cormorants and great egrets, with black-crowned night herons forming an outer ring in the lower trees.

With permission from local wildlife authorities, I sat for two days in a tree-top blind. Below me was an egret nest with two young, across from me a number of cormorant nests with youngsters grown enough to be adventuring out onto nearby branches, and above me a great blue heron nest with four scruffy topknots just visible over the edge.

One of the adult herons landed in a tree close to its nest. It studied the situation a few minutes, then with neck and legs outstretched, letting out a hoarse squawk, flew to its young. It was closely followed by its mate. The two raised their heads and necks straight up in what appeared to be a recognition or pair-bonding ceremony. The first bird flew off, and the one that had just returned regurgitated food for the young.

I didn't have to be very observant to notice when the parent cormorants returned. The young growled loudly as they teetered on slender branches, anxiously maneuvering to be the first to thrust their heads down the adults' throats for food.

The young pair of egrets appeared to have better manners. They rested low in the nest, occasionally standing and looking for their parents. However, when an elegant white adult did return, they were just as voracious and pushy about getting their meal as all the other birds.

Near sunset I left my vigil and watched the evening flights from my canoe. Great Vs of cormorants sailed in for the night, landing not only in the rookery, but roosting in other dead trees nearby as well. A line of white pelicans glided by just above water level and gracefully settled down on a mud flat.

I canoed slowly, with quiet strokes of my paddle. A doe and fawn came down to the shore. The doe stomped her hooves and blew a few short snorts at me, looking hard to detect movement. She uneasily climbed the bank, watched me a few seconds more,

The marsh dancers — western grebes

Great egret in breeding plumage

Trumpeter swan nesting on a muskrat house

Heron, egret, and cormorant rookery

then both she and her fawn bounded off with white tails flagging above the grasses.

White water-lily blossoms lay closed for the night, frogs were in full chorus, and the first bats of the evening were pursuing insects over the water.

As within any ecosystem, not only daily rhythms were unfolding, but also seasonal changes.

Already the water level had dropped significantly since the grebes had danced over the surface. Before long much of the marsh will have dried up, yellowlegs and marbled godwits will feed on mud flats, and the creatures of the water will either have to move to the deeper pools or burrow into the moist mud until fall rains or spring floods again replenish the waters.

Autumn will bring migrants from the north, huge flocks pausing to rest at the marsh and to feed in the nearby fields and prairies.

Muskrats will busy themselves securing their dome-shaped homes of cattails, which will be their late winter food supply as well as shelter. Beavers also will be adding to their lodges, but their winter food, branches, will be stuck into the bottom muck near their lodges. When they get hungry, they'll swim under the ice to the "forest" they've transplanted and bring a branch or piece of log back into the lodge for a meal of twigs and bark.

The winter landscape will be a bleak one compared to the abundance of the other seasons. Tracks in the snow will tell stories of mice and moles scurrying about, hunted by red fox and owls, but there will be little other evidence of life.

Beneath the blanket of snow and ice, oxygen-producing green plant growth will slow; dead plants and animals will decay, further robbing the water of oxygen. By the end of winter, life in the marsh will be at its lowest ebb, but the seeds of the past season will lie ready for a resurgence of growth that will begin when the first rays of sunshine penetrate the newly opened water.

Marsh-bordered pond, St. Croix River valley

Ring-necked ducks

Canada geese

Beaver pond, November

Snow-covered marsh tussocks

BOGS — THE SOUTH EDGE OF THE ARCTIC

Les

I was there at sunup that spring morning. The speckled alder swamp was a maze of one-to-three-inch-thick alder stems, tipped every which way, making me stoop under, climb over, or hang onto the alders while I long-stepped from one mossy hummock to the next.

One tends to walk off-balance on rotting logs rather than step into the black-water pools where the depth and footing are uncertain. Sometimes a misstep can mean a cold wetting. If you grasp a dead alder to swing around a clump of them to a moss-covered log and it breaks off in your hand, it isn't much help, and you're on your way down.

I was "earning my way" to a black spruce-tamarack bog by crossing an alder swamp "moat," the kind that surrounds many bogs and may be one of the reasons northern bogs are so seldom visited.

Most of these moats are not broad barriers, perhaps twenty-five to one hundred feet or so wide. But apparently they are discouraging enough to deter most hikers. In spite of the many superb pictures and interesting articles on bogs in nature-oriented magazines, in more than fifty years of frequent exploration, I have never met another person in a bog.

The border between alder swamp and spruce-tamarack bog is usually distinct. Once you have stepped onto the sphagnum moss base of the bog, you are there. And *there*, especially to a first-timer, is one of the best surprises in nature. The bog is not an alien world. It is a fun, friendly, fascinating place. If you fall, which you just might do on the springy hummocks, you *laugh*, because you fall on a soft mattress! Everything is "givey." It's like trying to walk on piles of rubber hot-water bottles half full of water. The moss is spongy, and it could be moist right under the surface in spring or after a rainy period. But in summer and fall it's dry and pleasant to flop down on and watch the clouds drift by.

If you've never been in a northern bog before, almost all of the plant life will be foreign to you. Apart from the black spruce and tamarack trees, which may be scattered and stunted or thick and fairly tall, most vegetation immediately apparent is low shrubbery.

On my dawn hike, as soon as I was across the

Pale laurel and bog rosemary bloom on the floating edge of the eye of a bog

alder swamp and onto the sphagnum, I was knee-deep in leatherleaf and Labrador tea, the most abundant bog shrubs found from northern Minnesota to Labrador and Alaska.

Shafts of early sun were poking through tiny holes in the tight spruce clumps and backlighting the translucent webwork done by yesterday's spiders. Every flower, leaf, and needle was sparkling with the night's dew. Were I not wearing hip boots, I'd have been soaked to the thighs.

I was searching for the "eye" of the bog, the pond or small lake that might still remain open on this type of bog, where floating vegetation grows toward the center from the edge and in time covers the entire pond. I had been there before, so I knew there was an open eye, but I had come from a different direction. By varying my approach I wouldn't be tempted to follow the same snowshoe hare trail, thus wearing a muddy path through the fragile mat of stems and roots. Also, I might find a rare orchid or plant that I'd miss if I walked the same route each time I came.

There were tightly clumped "islands" of black spruce and tamarack, and broad moss-and-shrub openings called muskegs. Fields of cotton grass were scattered over the bog, powder puffs on long stems that Craig and I have photographed in the Canadian Rockies and in Alaska.

The tree islands are like houses, with walls and roof of spruce and tamarack boughs. The inner tree trunks are shaded by their own crowns and by the surrounding walls, so there are bare trunks spaced quite evenly throughout the single room. I pushed through the springy, doorless wall of one of these island houses and stood in the cool, shaded interior. The floor was firm, green moss, thinly covered with copper brown needles. The room was not as empty as it first seemed. Three large, pink moccasin flowers were doing well in the cool shade, elegantly displayed at the edge of a yard-wide black pool. And one of my favorite flowers, goldthread, diminutive and charming, dappled the floor with its tiny white blossoms at one end of the columned room.

I was tempted to dawdle, to stay a while in that special place. But it was spring, and the eye was somewhere ahead.

Pushing out through boughs that swept the ground, I was again on the tumbly muskeg. I reckoned by the sun where the pond should be and wallowed on across the interwoven shrubs.

By a tiny clump of chest-high tamaracks I found a single rose pogonia. Finding just *one* of anything

makes me apprehensive. It might be the only one in that bog. The one-ness of it hurts more when the flower is as lovely as the rose pogonia, a graceful, showy pink orchid.

Ahead, beyond some scattered small islands, was several hundred feet of space to the next trees. Enough space so the distant colors were slightly muted. That broad opening must hold the eye.

I was right. As I stepped high over the leatherleaf and Labrador tea, I caught glimpses of blue water ahead. Rounding a last island, I was surrounded by pale laurel, that delicate pink shrub flower that also grows profusely in low mats above timberline in the Rockies. My several flower books identify it differently in English: pale laurel, bog laurel, swamp laurel; but it is *Kalmia polifolia* in all of them, so we know it is the same shrub. The tiny dark anthers are protected in small pockets in the petals until a bumblebee or other insect disturbs the flower. Then the curved stems snap the anthers out of the pockets and the pollen catches on the bee's hairy legs to be carried to other laurel blossoms for cross-pollination.

The edge of the eye alone makes a bog trip a delightful experience. From the last trees out to the edge of the pond, the bog is a floating bog. Literally, the land is floating on the water. I waded to within a few feet of the edge. With each step I depressed the floating mat until I was ankle-to-calf deep in water, and that same land floated up behind me as I walked on.

Sometimes I carry a canoe paddle, on a bog that is new to me, as a walking stick and to test the strength of the floating mat. If the vegetation is buoyant enough to hold me at the very edge of the eye and I can feel under the mat with the paddle and find only water, that is proof enough that the bog is really floating.

At an especially springy place, I "jumped" up and down in slow motion. Of course I couldn't really jump, because the "waterbed" mat went down instead of my going up, but I created *waves* across the bog. The nearest small tamarack trees, thirty feet away, went up and down in delayed reaction to my jumps.

After getting that kid stuff out of my system, I looked around on the floating bog for more familiar faces. Among the pink laurel were bog rosemary blossoms, waxy little white bells hanging on the underside of gracefully arched stems. Near the edge of the eye were the reddish purple flowers of marsh cinquefoil and the wedge-shaped leaves of sweetgale, both of which like wet feet and tundra; both are found in Alaska.

Pitcher plant leaves *are* pitchers. Curved like horns of plenty, with openings toward the sky, they are usually at least partially filled with rain water. Lined with hairs, with the nap leaning toward the water, the pitchers trap and drown enough insects to provide them with the nitrogen they need, not available in the acid soil of the bog.

Carefully searching on hands and knees, I found another carnivorous plant, the roundleaf sundew. The tiny round leaves, in a whorl around the flower stem at ground level, are covered with short hairs sticking straight out, each with a sweet, sticky drop at the end. An insect becoming stuck on one hair causes other gluey hairs to lean over and help enmesh it. This plant, too, has found a source of nitrogen in an acid environment.

I searched further. There was one special friend I still wanted to find to top off my spring visit to the eye. It is not an orchid, it is not even uncommon, but it is such an attractive little flower that I delight in finding it again each year. I wish it had a more poetic name; somehow *buckbean* does not describe the delicate beauty of *Menyanthes trifoliata*. Like tiny Easter lilies enhanced with white lace, these neat little blossoms bring me to my knees each time I happen upon them. On that day I did find just a few buckbeans, and they put sweet frosting on an already very tasty cake.

I seem to have made a big thing of the little (thirty acres or so) bog. Well, being a Minnesotan, I should tout our bogs! We are blessed with the most and the biggest, outside of Alaska, and considering the diverse bog terrain in at least one bog, the best.

How many? I have just unrolled the geological survey map of the area in which we live, and I can count at least eight spruce-tamarack bogs within the square mile that surrounds our home. Looking further, the entire two hundred miles of the Bruno Quadrangle (our area) has only a few sections of land without the familiar little swamp designations here and there. Neighboring maps (Holyoke, Danbury) are similarly marked.

If the Minnesota north woods averages only one bog per square mile, there are at least thirty thousand bogs in our state. I think that number would be very conservative. These vary from little half-dozen-tree pockets to bogs of several square miles and way on up to the largest of all northern bogs in the contiguous states, the Big Bog.

The nearest bog on our land, just minutes from our house, is "part of the family." We show it off to friends and "go see how it is" often. Our most frequent contact is an everyday visit, not actually with the bog but with a stream fed by it. The bog is a small one, only a few acres, but it has a profound effect on the stream. In spring, the flow is steady long after the snow melts. If we get two to three inches of rain within a couple of days, the stream rises but does not overflow its banks, nor does it run dirty. It has a good, clear flow for many days after the rain.

The water-holding capacity of thousands of bogs on Minnesota's streams and rivers is graphic. A constant flow of clear North Shore rivers can be counted on for waterfall extravaganzas during all but the driest times. The St. Louis River watershed is smaller than you'd think when you see that roaring spring cataract through Jay Cooke State Park, but the bog-evened flow is constant enough that it is used for hydroelectric power.

In contrast, virtually all field-bordered streams in agricultural regions run brown after a pouring rainstorm, then dry up.

The slow, steady flow from the bogs keeps beaver ponds full, providing habitat not only for the beavers but also for ducks, mergansers, grebes, herons, bitterns, kingfishers, ospreys, redwings, moose, mink, muskrats, otters, turtles, frogs, fish, and more.

The woodcutting of the beavers lets sunshine reach the forest floor, growing new aspens and browse shrubs, enhancing habitat for deer, moose, ruffed grouse, and songbirds. When the beavers are trapped, or move after they have cut all of the aspens near their pond, the dam disintegrates and the pond drains. It is replaced by a meadow of sedges and grasses, good habitat for mice, voles, shrews, and some ground-nesting birds. Foxes and coyotes hunt these meadows. So do hawks and owls. Bears graze on the plant life. Tree and shrub species reseed in the meadows, providing more browse for deer and moose. In the meantime aspens are growing rapidly above the floodplain. In fifteen to twenty-five years they will be able to support another beaver colony, and the cycle will start again.

The spruce-tamarack bogs are home to many kinds of birds and animals that are not found elsewhere and to some that are also found on higher ground. Caribou used to roam the Minnesota bogs. Their broad hooves evolved to support them on soft muskeg and tundra. Perry Swedberg, an early state forest ranger, told me

Calypso orchid, Chippewa National Forest

Buckbean

when I was a boy that he saw a caribou not far from his town of Malmo, on Mille Lacs Lake, when he was young. Highway 65 passes through Solana State Forest near there, and that bog area is picture-perfect caribou country.

Neighbor-naturalist Bob Eikum photographed a great gray owl in summer in a spruce-tamarack bog near his home. We can continue to expect that species of birds and animals that nest or live in the subarctic will be recorded in Minnesota. Our bogs are, in both appearance and vegetation, the south edge of the arctic.

When you drive almost any highway or road through the north woods, you pass spruce-tamarack bogs quite often. The black spruces that are actually in the cold bog (not those affected by the warm soil of ditch banks) almost all look stunted, even though they might be thirty or more feet tall. Often there is foliage just in the top few feet of the tree, and the annual growth at the end of the branches is but two or three inches. This gives a bunchy irregularity to many spruces in contrast with "church steeple" balsams.

Tamaracks have a loose, feathery look in summer; their needles are in little puffs along the branches rather than evenly spaced like spruce or balsam. The tamarack is the only Minnesota conifer that drops all its needles in winter. They look quite dead among the green spruces, but their reddish brown branches are very much alive and will leaf out come spring.

Some of the bogs along northern Minnesota's roads are quite extensive. U.S. 2 from Duluth to Bemidji goes through many bogs of mixed types, some with solid spruce-tamarack forests, some with well-spaced, stunted trees, and others with open muskeg with large fields of cotton grass, laurel, and many other bog flowers. U.S. 210 from Brainerd to Duluth is another good bog road. So are State 73 and U.S. 53 north to the Iron Range. The truth is, almost any north-woods road will take you past or through many northern bogs. That doesn't necessarily mean you can park and step out into one to see what it's like. Most road ditches that parallel bogs are quite deep and full of water. If you do want to visit a bog, take high rubber boots, look for a shallow ditch, carry a compass and know how to use it.

The Big Bog

Until now we've been talking about some mighty fine bogs, each with a whole new world to offer first-time visitors. The bog section of this book could end here, and I'd be happy to have enticed some of you to try a new experience that I think you'd like.

But if I didn't tell you about the BIG one, I'd be leaving out a phenomenon that is truly one of the wonders of our state. Actually, it is a national treasure, a one-of-a-kind.

The Big Bog, north and east of Red Lake, belongs to all of us. Most of it is within the borders of large tracts of state land: Beltrami Island State Forest, Red Lake State Wildlife Management Area, Pine Island State Forest, and Koochiching State Forest.

The Big Bog is a million acres big, the same size as the Boundary Waters Canoe Area Wilderness. It is the largest continuous body of peatland in the lower forty-eight states.

In 1975, 137,920 acres of peatland in the Red Lake Wildlife Area (part of the Big Bog) were placed on the National Registry of Natural Landmarks by the United States Department of the Interior.

The Minnesota Department of Natural Resources Scientific and Natural Areas Section has included the Red Lake Peatland in its registry system of areas with unique and rare resources of high significance to the natural diversity of Minnesota.

The difference between the Big Bog and the thousands of smaller bogs across northern Minnesota can best be seen from the air. From high above, the Big Bog becomes a unit, all connected and each part contributing to the whole. A huge, many-tubed funnel drawing water from hundreds of square miles, the bog is a graceful mosaic of fen-bog water courses (thin floating mats of sedges and sphagnum moss with associated plants) and variously shaped islands and broad sections of boreal trees and shrubs. I'm worried that tampering with any part of this grand, living flowage might affect the entire complex.

It is no wonder the bog is big. It is growing on part of the lake bed of Glacial Lake Agassiz, which covered two hundred thousand square miles at its maximum extent. Lake Superior, by comparison, is thirty-one thousand square miles.

The Big Bog is the most southerly expression of patterned peatland in North America. It is almost identical to the true boreal patterned peatland of the far north, found in the northernmost forested land around the world.

One needs a whole new vocabulary to converse in Big Bog. A Big Bog person talks about

Mushrooms and pitcher plants growing in sphagnum moss

Strangmoors, fens, ericaceous shrubs and *muskeg* (*semiumbrogenous* mosses). That person might even mention a weakly *soligenous* poor bog, or share with us an exciting moment when he almost drowned in a *flark.*

Most of these strange words we'll just laugh at and forget. But there is one, *paludification*, that intrigues me. Most of us who have heard of bogs at all have seen the classic drawings in cross section of a floating bog closing over a pond. So most of us probably think that that is the only way bogs are formed.

In my reading about the Big Bog, I came upon *paludification.* That means that a good bog moss, sphagnum, takes root and starts growing on a suitable base, and just keeps growing deeper and deeper, upon itself. Due to its remarkable ability to absorb and hold water, it lifts the water table as it grows. Much of the Big Bog is a layer of peat and moss that grows thicker each year due to paludification.

Miron "Bud" Heinselman, forestry expert, who has done in-depth studies of the Big Bog, told me of his very interesting findings at Myrtle Lake in the Lake Agassiz Peatland Natural Area, in Koochiching County. Myrtle is one of the rare lakes left when Lake Agassiz receded, and it has been in continuous existence since then. Mosses started their upward growth on the old Agassiz lake bed in the Myrtle Lake area about 5,000 years ago, and around Myrtle Lake itself, only 2,700 years ago. Since then the bog has raised steadily around Myrtle Lake, and *so has the lake.* As the sphagnum raised the water table around the lake, it also raised the lake itself at least 11.8 feet. Can you imagine anything as porous and soft as moss and peat holding a 160-acre lake on a slope? The bottom of the lake is now higher than the surface was when the bog started its upward growth. The entire lake is now higher than the mineral ridge that originally impounded it, and is dammed by moss and peat alone.

If *wildness* means "seldom if ever walked on by people," the Big Bog vies with the Boundary Waters (away from the lakes and trails) and other remote sections of the state for the honor of being wildest of all.

For instance, if I were to leave the state campground at Waskish and drive north on Minnesota Highway 72 about eight or ten miles, park, and think of hiking straight west to the next road, FORGET IT! First of all, the deep, water-filled roadside ditch would be a major deterrent. But let's say that I do get across the ditch. It is thirty to thirty-five miles to the next road, bog and fen all the way. That is the same distance as the length of the famous Kekekabic Trail in the Boundary Waters, but in the Big Bog there is no trail.

There are more deterrents. From 1909 to 1917, there were drainage projects in the Big Bog to make farming feasible and attract homesteaders. Fifteen hundred miles of drainage ditches approximately ten to twenty feet wide and six to ten feet deep were dug following section lines. The bog won. Poor soil, ineffective drainage, fires, and no nearby markets drove discouraged homesteaders out.

Aspens, balsam poplars, and other beaver fare grew on the drier ditch banks, and beavers established colonies across the bog that stopped or slowed the drainage. Beavers have an aversion to running water. On the Beltrami County map I find seven old ditches I'd have to cross on beaver dams in the first twelve miles of my across-the-bog trek.

Beyond the last ditch, I would be walking across fens and bogs through another twenty miles of wilderness. This is uncertain footing at best. Conservation officer Greg Spaulding, bog enthusiast and orchid photographer, has broken through the thin net of roots when walking across a fen in search of orchids. He said the water was frigid in mid-summer, kept cold by the insulating moss.

Fen-bogs — low growth, mostly floating mats of sedges and sphagnum — are treeless water-flow passages through the bog. Some are twenty-five miles or more long and up to four miles wide. There are tear-drop-shaped spruce and tamarack islands scattered on these fens with round ends upstream and long points downstream, like a school of whales swimming up a broad river. Most of these whale-shaped islands are from a quarter- to a half-mile long.

Larger islands, a mile or more wide and several miles long, are fitted into the flow pattern in many odd shapes. Most of these are also pointed on the downstream end and may be covered with spruce, tamarack, white cedar, or a mixture of shrubs. Some spruce islands have many points, patterned somewhat like frost crystals on a window. I asked Bud Heinselman, my forester friend, what caused the strange jagged edges on these islands. The answer I would never have guessed. The islands are on a divide between Red Lake and the Rainy River, and the points show the direction of water flow; a

Black spruce

dramatic effect from what must be an almost unmeasurable, gentle flow within the first few rods of the divide, where the land all looks absolutely flat!

The bog and fen land is so fragile that trails can be seen for years after use had ceased. On most of the bog no signs of human visitation are visible from the air. Trails attributed to the last caribou herd in the state (in the 1940s) are still discernible from a helicopter.

Afterthought

As so often is the case in nature, what seems to have happened accidentally during millions of years of evolution turns out to be an excellent working part of the whole ecosystem. Floodplains are a case in point. They have developed "that way" through time because of "accidental" circumstances. The valley bottoms were filled in by erosion, creating flat bottomlands. Plants, shrubs, and trees evolved that could withstand the periodic flooding of those muddy flats. Spring floodwaters spread over the floodplains, where they were absorbed, slowed down and cleaned, then released slowly to ease the flooding downstream.

Humankind, accepting dry periods as "normal," not only farmed the floodplains but built cities on them, which, of course, have been flooded frequently. So people built dikes to protect the cities, keeping water *off* the floodplains. With nothing to slow it down, floodwater sluiced downstream in a hurry. Because the upstream people were funneling spring meltwater off the land all at once, higher dikes had to be built downstream, and so on down the river.

Minnesota's spruce-tamarack bogs are serving so quietly as giant reservoirs to gradually release water that I'm worried they might be destroyed before we know how valuable they are.

Will bogs be mined for peat? Will peat-dependent fuel industries be so big that they must use up most of our large bogs to be "economically feasible"?

Are we again going to go for the quick gain and then kick ourselves because we goofed? Compared to all possible sources of energy, Minnesota's peat would be a small, nonrenewable source for a relatively small number of consumers for a relatively short time. The cost would be the destruction of ecological treasures that we are just now beginning to appreciate.

THE NORTH SHORE

Les

It is 2:33 A.M., August 2. The temperature is in the mid-forties. Yesterday afternoon as I drove up the North Shore, Duluth radio reported forty-eight degrees at the same time it was ninety-one hot, muggy degrees in the Twin Cities.

I've been lying awake listening to a powerful, pulsating surf, trying to analyze the sounds. That's one of the nicer things about tent walls — they let you hear the night sounds.

Even so, I had to get up and out, to stare down between the birch trunks here at cliff edge until I could see the great combers fan out around the rocky point below me. But it was the *sounds* that woke me, that shook my shoulders and got me up. What are they saying? Can I discern, describe, spell what I am hearing?

Certainly there is a constant roar, constant in that it does not stop. But even the word *pulsating*, the first word that came to me, is not accurate, because the rhythm, if there is one, is so spread as the great mounds and crests hit the uneven cliffs and bays that the beat is lost to me.

At any one place there is certainly a rhythm, the big swells sloshing higher every seventh wave or so, and really striking high and sending spray far inland about every twenty-first wave, with three or four good ones in a row.

I stopped along the scenic route between Duluth and Two Harbors yesterday to experience the high surf, and amid the wave-splashed rocks found a relatively dry boulder. Some quirk kept the spray away from my vantage point, and that variance in rock structure gave me an excellent seat for a spectacular show. For the first time in my life I saw sizable stones being flung up in the exploding spray. That was a hard place to leave.

It somehow seems fitting that I am writing this in the warm quiet glow of a fat candle as exciting sounds fill the air around me. I hear whoosh . . . whoosh . . . whoosh . . . from the point below, but also from other points and beaches in rhythms not tied to this one. And there's an occasional *ka-whump!* from the other side of this headland and from the cliffs to the west. A low, booming bass is almost constant behind it all.

Out there, from cliff edge, I saw the lights of a passing ship, dimmed to a ghostlike glow by the twenty miles or so between us. I could perceive its downlake movement when I lined it up with the thick trunk of a tree. The ship's smallness in that vast darkness somehow emphasized the wildness of the lake more than if it had not been there.

I could see no other lights of civilization, not even a glow in the sky. Much of the North Shore is still wild. And even though many tourists drive Highway 61 during the brief summers, that road is still just a narrow thread in a spacious wilderness. It does not cut off the inland wild from the lake. Hundreds of deer move to the shore in winter to take advantage of the relative warmth near the water, the shallower snow, and the numerous browse shrubs amid the shelter of balsams and cedars. Timber wolves follow the deer and sometimes pursue them out onto the ice when the lake is frozen. Moose and lynx, fishers and bears, all visit the shore.

Yesterday afternoon, driving north on Interstate 35 from our rural Moose Lake home, I could see hilly, almost mountainous terrain miles before reaching Duluth. Those granite mounds are the southwest extremity of the Sawtooth Range, the timbered hills which parallel the North Shore. Climbing a long grade through open country, I could look back to my right across a broad valley of unbroken forest. The St. Louis River is down there, hidden in a deep fold, miles of white water roaring through the upended rock of Jay Cooke State Park.

The freeway continues up into the hills to a high, rolling plateau of sugar maple woods. It stays up there long enough for you to forget how high you are, when suddenly you are given some choices: you can continue on Interstate 35 and drop down into the city of Duluth, or you can turn right or left on the Skyline Parkway to drive along wild forest roads to spectacular overlooks. This time, with visiting the North Shore the primary reason for my trip, I continued on the freeway. And there it was — the grand view of the city, the harbor, the famous Aerial Lift Bridge, Minnesota Point, and beyond it all, the deep blue of Lake Superior.

I did take time to revisit Minnesota Point, to again get the feel of that seven-mile-long sand bar that separates the Duluth-Superior Harbor from Lake Superior. Turning right on Lake Street, I crossed the Aerial Lift Bridge and drove several miles to the parking circle at the end of the road. From there on, the point is wild. There is a miles-long fine sand beach on the Lake Superior side, where one can often walk alone, especially on a cool day. The dunes are held in check by grasses, shrubs, and sedges. Even though the seed sources may be hundreds of miles away, seeds of anchoring plants somehow find drifting sand, take root, and slow or stop the movement. A narrow forest of pines further anchors the point. Like an ocean reef, Minnesota Point protects the quiet harbor from storms on the big lake.

When I was a college student in Duluth, we flushed prairie chickens from the dunes on botany field trips. The beach is a top-notch birding spot for shorebirds, some seldom seen elsewhere in the state. Lucky spring birders can sometimes see dozens of the dapper ruddy turnstones there. Viewed from the beach on Minnesota Point, the high North Shore dwindles to a needle point and then to zero as your eyes follow that shore northeast toward Canada. By road it is more than six hundred miles along the North Shore to the far end of the lake. As a string is stretched across a map, Minnesota Point is closer to the Nebraska border than it is to the other end of Lake Superior.

As I drive northeast out of Duluth across the Lester River, I often get a twinge of wanting to turn around and drive up the east end of Skyline Parkway to Hawk Ridge. That rather ordinary looking pull-off has special status, not for viewing the scenery below, but as what just might be the best place in the world for viewing raptors, the taloned predator birds. The North Shore of Lake Superior, slanting from northeast to southwest, acts like a giant wedge, collecting hawks and eagles (and turkey vultures) as they reach the shore on their southward fall migration and steering them around the end of the big lake at Duluth. The Sawtooth Range, paralleling the shore, gives these birds the updrafts on which they can ride, hunt, and play for more than 250 miles from the northernmost shore of the lake to Hawk Ridge.

Many watchers come great distances to view this rare and spectacular show and are sometimes rewarded with one-day totals of thousands of hawks. The best day to go there, at about the same time fall color hits its peak, is *yesterday*. "You should have been here — ." At least that seems to be my experience as to when the highest numbers of birds and species are seen.

Often from a few to dozens of hawks are seen circling in "kettles," updrafts that they ride with outstretched wings, spiraling higher and higher until they find a favorable wind to ride to the next kettle. But more exciting are the times the big birds almost take your cap off as they skim up the slope barely over your head as they sail or flap by.

Earlier this summer I was here at this same campground at Kennedy's Landing on a rare warm night. Even then I was impressed by the weather-making power of Lake Superior. A hundred feet inland the night was balmy — sport-shirt weather. But here at my campsite twenty feet from cliff edge (a vertical drop of about

Lake Superior, near Hovland

Mouth of the Beaver River

Herring gull

Palisade Head

White spruce, Shovel Point

Manitou Falls

Mountain ash

Northern hardwoods, Sawtooth Range, from Mount Oberg

Upper falls of the Brule River

Paper birches, Lester River area, Duluth

Fly amanita, Judge C. R. Magney State Park

Susie Islands from Mount Josephine

Lake Superior shoreline near Tettegouche State Park

Cascade River

Ice formations near the mouth of the Cascade River

twenty feet to the lake), a slight air movement from the lake would lower the temperature to heavy-wool-sweater cold within a few seconds. And just as quickly, a breath of air from inland would warm me to short-sleeve comfort.

Growing up within forty miles of the big lake, I have been aware of the hug airconditioner all of my life. Often there is a sharp temperature difference near Rutledge, fifty miles south from Minnesota Point, with weather in the eighties or nineties south of the line and the low fifties north of it.

When you think of the bulk of that massive lake, more than 31,000 square miles, 1,300 feet deep at its deepest point, with the temperature around it below freezing nearly half of each year, it's no wonder that its coldness reaches out to affect the surrounding land in summer and that its relative warmness moderates the shore temperature in winter.

The North Shore — where the world's largest freshwater lake borders sheer cliffs, a mountain range, long curves of beaches, and a rich boreal forest — has to hold Minnesota's most fabulous scenery. Any two of the above would attract artists; the potential of all five presents limitless beauty.

But there is more. Imagine finding a bonsai spruce at cliff edge, 120 feet above the water, with curtains of fog playing lovely visual tricks with the rugged shore far below.

Imagine being alone, or with someone very special, experiencing wild surf, where pelting spray slaps you hard or a foaming wave sloshes around your ankles but you don't care because you're dressed for it.

Imagine hiking up a canyon-walled trout stream, coming to an apparent boxed-in dead end, then rounding a sharp bend and finding a classic waterfall.

I did all of that this summer at Shovel Point, Cascade State Park, and Kodonce River State Wayside.

I hiked to the top of Mount Josephine to look out across the Susie Islands. Seven hundred feet above the lake, I had a grand view of the Susies, Pigeon Point — that long, wild, easternmost tip of our state — and Isle Royale National Park,

twenty-two miles from where I stood. A surprising fact about the "north-ness" of Pigeon Point — the closest wild polar bears are nearer than is Des Moines, Iowa.

The Susies are often fog covered when the mainland is clear. In addition to fog, their exposure to storms and surf has maintained differences from the mainland through the centuries that make these wild islands very special. They even differ from each other. Some will support northern white cedar, others only spruce. The forest floor is deep with billows of reindeer moss (really a lichen), and old granddaddy's beard festoons dead branches. Crowberries and several other species of plants found on the arctic tundra are also growing on the Susies. That fact is unusual enough that The Nature Conservancy has acquired a sanctuary there.

The many North Shore streams fed by abundant rainfall and the dramatic drop in elevation in the last mile or so to the lake have resulted in a wonderland of waterfalls, from tinkling rivulets to roaring, free-falling, mist-shrouded cataracts. Six state parks and four state waysides feature North Shore streams and rivers.

The Cascade River is about as picturesque as a stream can be, with waterfalls alternating right and left as an artist would place them, gracefully dropping into deep, black pools, framed with fresh, green fronds of white cedar.

My wife, Fran, and I have a special love for that place. We camped there before it was a park, on our honeymoon. And I camped at Cascade for two months one winter while making a deer movie.

I witnessed the unbelievable power of a light wind on thousands of square miles of ice as the great sheets kept coming, unslowed by the ancient granite shore. Folding and piling, the roaring, screeching, tinkling mass became a dazzling heap of sparkles, mostly diamond white but some red, blue, and gold, separated by prism fractures.

This was also prepark. It was wilder then. No one visited my camp up beyond the falls except one game warden. He left a note on the snow between my balsam-bough bed and my food cache. "I visited your camp on February 10, 1948. Art Allen, Game Warden."

THE GREAT NORTH WOODS

Les

B*oreal.* The word itself stirs my blood. It's every use spells romance. The boreal forest, aurora borealis, even King Boreas of the St. Paul Winter Carnival — all sing the song of the north wind.

And that is where it started. In Greek mythology, Eos, goddess of dawn, wife of Astraeus, bore the stars and the winds. The north wind was called Boreas.

Today, the word *boreal* has broadened to mean northern. My dictionary states it thus: "of, relating to, or growing in northern and mountainous parts of the northern hemisphere."

The boreal forest in North America extends from central Alaska, where the scattered black and white spruce of the taiga are in sufficient numbers and close enough together to be called forest, east across Canada to the maritime provinces and New England. The southern edge of this broad forest drops down into northern Minnesota, Wisconsin, and Michigan. The name now also implies that this forest is composed of coniferous (cone-bearing) trees. The Minnesota section of the boreal forest contains not only the same species of spruce and tamarack as those in Alaska, but also white, red, and jack pines, balsam fir, and white cedar. In my opinion the epitome of beauty, the lush growth, variety of species, and magnificent settings of the boreal forest are found on both sides of the Minnesota-Ontario border from Rainy Lake to Lake Superior.

Here in Minnesota not only the northern lights and the boreal forest keep the god Boreas alive, but also the lovely flowers *Clintonia borealis* and *Linnaea borealis* (twin flower), the boreal chickadee, with a brown cap instead of black, and the boreal owl, a rare winter visitor to our north woods.

Other birds and many animals say boreal forest without actually spelling it out. The spruce grouse's handsome dark suit is safely inconspicuous in the northern coniferous forest. Our national bird, the bald eagle, nests in the crowns of northern Minnesota's tall white pines. The raven, the gray jay, and the black-backed woodpecker are present all year. The osprey and its hawk cousins come north to nest, but like many Minnesotans, go south for the winter.

Brilliant little jewels of birds, the warblers, are just the opposite of camouflaged in northern evergreens, in their showy breeding plumage. Two of my favorites are the black-throated green and the flashy blackburnian. A real bonanza of black-throated greens flitted after insects near the dock at YMCA Camp Menogyn when I was there.

One evening a number of years ago, shortly

before sunset, I was high on a rugged outcrop looking down on McFarland Lake. Earlier in the day, farther up the hill, I sat stone-still while a buck with exceptionally large antlers browsed to within a few yards of me. It was a quiet day with but slight air movement from the buck to me. The only sounds were the almost inaudible snaps as he jerked twigs loose that he hadn't completely cut. He never did notice me.

As good sunsets do, that one deepened to rich reds and golds, pinks and violets. The lake below was set deep between the surrounding hills, and the sunset colors were even more vivid reflected in the mirror-calm water.

I turned to see the effect of the warm light on the forested hill behind me, and my eyes were immediately drawn to a cliff like the one I was on, perhaps one-hundred-fifty feet above me. There, at cliff edge, stood a handsome timber wolf, looking out across the lake as I had been doing. Did he appreciate sunsets, too? He apparently had also been watching me, because he did not look down at me when I turned around. Instead, he continued to stand unmoving, the creamy parts of his coat shining gold. Then when he was ready, he lowered his head and turned it slightly to look directly at me, stared for a few precious seconds, and was gone.

With the buck and the wolf still pumping adrenaline into the exuberance section of my brain, it was hard to give just another gorgeous sunset the attention and appreciation it deserved.

When the white man first came to Minnesota, the boreal forest covered much more of the state than it does now. Within a few decades much of the state was logged. Severe fires through tinder-dry slashings and frequent fires without effective fire-fighting equipment burned the soil itself and killed seedlings. The seed source was destroyed. Much of the former evergreen forest is now birch-aspen, and most of the mixed pine-hardwoods no longer have the big pine plumes above the maples and basswoods.

The true boreal forest, over much of the state where it was formerly found, is gone for now.

But there are still some tall remnant pines. There are fine second- and third-growth pines in the sand country, there are lots of balsams in many areas under the aspens, and there are still many spruce-tamarack bogs. The northeastern third of the state is still the north woods to most of us.

And to a very enthusiastic group of young people that Craig and I met at Lac La Croix, it is The *Great*

North Woods. We were on our way back from a sixteen-day canoe trip when we met the group at sundown. They invited us to eat with them and to camp nearby. They warned us that they would be leaving about four o'clock the next morning because they were due back at base camp that day.

We slept soundly and were unaware of any camp activity until they were ready to shove off in their loaded canoes. Then — "IT'S GOOD TO BE ALIVE IN THE GREAT NORTH WOODS!" thundered out in a many-voiced chorus through the wilderness. And it was!

For many years it seemed that man was bent on eliminating not only the north-woods forest itself, but many of the living things associated with that forest. Many furbearers were trapped to extinction or nearly so. Moose were overhunted until 1924, when hunting was stopped because there were so few left. Homesteaders tried to farm land that could not support farming. The showy lady's slipper, our state flower, and other orchids were picked or transplanted until most were gone.

But with better fire protection, controlled harvest of trees, more responsible game laws, and an enlightened citizenry practicing conservation and interested in ecology, some good things are happening now in the north woods.

Much of the logged and burned forest is now tall and handsome second growth. The brown-furred, mink-sized marten, who can race through the treetops and catch red squirrels, is now back in the state. So is the larger, darker fisher, who catches and eats martens! The timber wolf, placed on the endangered species list, has rebounded strongly. Moose have multiplied in such numbers that they are again hunted in the state. Lynxes are back and even a caribou (Hovland, 1980, photographed by Bill Peterson, state biologist). If a wolverine in Minnesota has not been confirmed by the time this book has gone to press, I have a feeling that one will be shortly.

Canoe Country

From my statement at a congressional hearing on the Boundary Waters Canoe Area in St. Paul in 1978, I have selected a few thoughts that I'd like to share with you:

"When I was a boy, road maps of Minnesota contained a statement in very fine print among some bits of blue between Ely and Grand Marais. The statement read, 'World's Greatest and Only Exclusive Canoe Country.' Even that long ago, the

Boreal forest, Little Saganaga Lake, BWCAW

Fire-killed trees

Balsam firs and sugar maples

Water-lily pads, Caribou Lake

Seagull River

area was recognized for what it should be — *the world's greatest and only exclusive canoe country.*

"When I was sixteen I went on my first canoe trip and fell in love with the Superior-Quetico. Even then I was saying, 'When I die, scatter my ashes under these pines. I want to become part of all this!' That was forty years ago . . .

"What is this great canoe country around which so many battles have been fought?

"It is a thousand island-filled lakes, like strings of beads connected by tumbling streams. It is high cliffs and great boulders and gently sloping granite beaches by campsites.

"It is paddling into a good breeze with eyes wide open and never getting a speck of dust in the eye.

"It is lichens and mosses, ferns and orchids, and a thin layer of moss-covered soil over granite, supporting seven kinds of evergreens, birches, aspens, and a scattering of red maples for flaming accent in the fall.

"It's getting up at the crack of dawn for a silent paddling stalk along the shore before breakfast, slipping along as quietly as the fog itself, hoping to see mink, beaver, bear, deer, or moose . . ."

When Congress voted to give most of the Boundary Waters Canoe Area wilderness status in 1978, many Minnesotans' hearts beat considerably slower. They didn't uncross their fingers, but they would sleep easier for a while at least.

The Superior-Quetico Canoe Country has been guarded against despoliation by a succession of champions through decades of time and an almost endless series of threats. Logging, hydroelectric power dams, roads to develop every lake, unlimited seaplane invasion, mining, unlimited motorboat and snowmobile use, all were fought off, and *any* of them would have spoiled the fresh, clean, wild beauty of this fragile wilderness.

Who were these champions? Ernest Oberholtzer saw that this international lakeland wilderness was one-of-a-kind and in danger of being lost to exploitation as early as the 1920s. He was heard, and he helped found the Wilderness Society in 1935. He was on the society's governing council for more than thirty years, working tirelessly toward seeing his vision of a Superior-Quetico canoe wilderness become a reality.

Colorful storyteller and canoe guide Bill Magie surveyed much of what is now the BWCAW when it was still relatively little used. He fell in love with that land, guided many famous people through it, and founded Friends of the Boundary Waters to back up that love with action.

Author Sigurd F. Olson endeared thousands of people to the Boundary Waters through his books. Readers far into the future will know and love this precious land through *The Singing Wilderness, Listening Point, Runes of the North,* and the others. Sig was president of the Wilderness Society, adviser to several administrations of government on wilderness matters, and an almost worshipped lecturer as he proclaimed his love of the land in sensitive poetic prose.

Bud Heinselman has done so much more than go "the extra mile" as his "bit" to add the *W* (for Wilderness) to the BWCA. Through his work as an ecologist with the United States Forest Service, he gained broad recognition as the top expert on the role of fire in the Boundary Waters boreal forest. Like the others, Bud also lost his heart to this magnificent land of rock, lakes, and pines. The final battle to gain full protection for the BWCA was coming up fast, and Bud had to be a part of it. He retired from his job with the forest service, rented with his wife, Fran, an apartment in Washington, D.C., and worked from there for two years. He gathered like minds to form the Friends of the Boundary Waters Wilderness and was the articulate voice of that group through the long and trying ordeal.

The threats and the champions stirred action by caring people all across the country, many who may never see the Boundary Waters but feel that it is right that this special area be saved. Hearings were crowded, many moving letters were sent to congressmen, and lots of people gave "'til it hurt" again and again.

Why? The people themselves said it. Many used the word *unique.* Nowhere else on earth is there a wilderness of thousands of interconnected lakes so uniquely right for canoe travel. Paddle routes weave among wooded islands, down narrow waterways, and alongside granite cliffs. Paintings left on these cliffs by Native Americans say someone was here hundreds of years ago who treated the land gently. Now, almost unbelievably, much of it is still as unspoiled as it was then.

There are more than a million acres in the BWCAW, and a like amount in adjacent Quetico Provincial Park in Canada. Through most of this canoe wilderness there is *only* wilderness upstream to the height of land, so I dip my cup alongside the canoe and drink the sweet, clear water.

In spite of the fact that big-pine logging started in what is now the Boundary Waters in 1895, 540,000 acres of true wilderness remain, never having been

Bunchberry

Little Rock Falls

Showy lady's slippers

Boulders along Horse Portage

Honey mushrooms, pipsissewa, and bunchberry

Common Loon

Seagull Lake

invaded by road or saw. Considering the odds against that happening when you know the history of the area, this has been an enormous accomplishment. The BWCAW contains the largest virgin forest in the eastern United States. Together with the totally protected land across the border in Quetico Park, there are over a million acres of contiguous virgin country in the international canoe wilderness.

The Boundary Waters and the woods around our house are the two places in this world where I feel most at home.

I first canoed the boundary waters in 1937, with my father and game warden Charlie Ott — from Poplar Lake down through Liz, Caribou, Horseshoe, Gaskin, Winchell, Trap, Grassy, Mulligan, Lily and Brule, then up through the Cones, Cliff, Winchell, beautiful Omega, Hensen, Pillsbury, Allen, Caribou, and back to Poplar. A forty-two inch northern pike, a mother bear and three cubs, a swimming buck stopping to look back after climbing the bank, filing the barbs off our hooks so we could release a succession of four-to-six-pound northerns easier, Charlie throwing his hat at a "porky" to get me some quills — those are just a few of the incidents on that first trip that sold me on Canoe Country. And on Charlie Ott, a lifelong friend and a companion of many good times in the wilds.

Fran and I gave ourselves a canoe for a wedding present and paddled from Gunflint to Big Saganaga on our honeymoon. It being the end of October and the first week of November, we unsurprisingly saw no one else on the trip. When we discovered that our meat supply was still being kept cold and fresh in my mother's refrigerator at Moose Lake, I played the hero, and we lived (partially) off the country.

On the portage to Clove Lake, I was making my second trip over the portage when Fran came running to meet me. She had our gun with her and a couple of shells (that was the only time I've carried a gun in Canoe Country). She had seen a ruffed grouse and tried to put our little double-barreled shotgun together but didn't know how. I did, the grouse was still there, and we had partridge stew on what Fran called our "wedding cake" island. The sun set and a full orange harvest moon came up at the same time to help us celebrate that special meal.

We camped the next night on a sand beach. There were no insects with the frosty nights and the weather was clear, so we slept in the open. Just as we awoke the next morning, three black ducks came diving over us from inland. As soon as they cleared the trees, they dropped steeply, their wings slicing the air with loud whooshes as they tipped right and left. They settled in lightly, flapped a couple of times, and swam around right out in front of us. There was dinner, and the gun was still in the canoe. I waited until the ducks swam down the shore and into some rushes at the mouth of a stream, then dressed and followed. With my city bride of four days watching, I crept down the shore on one hand and knees to the edge of the rushes. I gathered my legs under me, pressed off the safety, and slowly stood up, shivering from the cold and hoping to not look totally incompetent. The ducks flushed within range and just about where I thought they'd be. Two dropped. I tried to act nonchalant as I paddled out to pick up my prizes, but I almost had buck fever *after* the fact. I'm really not that good a shot.

Two gray jays watched from a few feet away as I cleaned the ducks. I found some flat, thin rocks and built what I thought was an ingenious oven, in which the flames heat a slab from underneath, then go up in back and are directed forward over the food. It worked fine, if you like your ducks a bit black on top. Later in the trip a four-pound northern pike provided fish courses for two meals.

Two days after we returned home we had fourteen inches of snow on the ground, and none of it melted until the next March.

As often as I have looked at our dozens of canoe maps, I am still impressed by the vast, interconnected maze of blue lakes. The old standard Fisher book of fifteen canoe maps gives me devastating one-upmanship material against anyone from anywhere touting his or her lake country. But the two maps that are most apt to cause a stranger to shake a head in disbelief are the large ones centering on Big Saganaga to the east and Basswood to the west.

I have those maps in front of me now, and it's as if all the world's lakes were gathered on this one-hundred-ten-mile stretch straddling the Minnesota-Ontario border.

As my eyes wander around the lakes and follow the dotted-line portages, I can relive priceless moments from forty-five years of pack, paddle, and portage, such as:

On the coming-home end of a sixteen-day loop to Chatterton Falls, Craig and I came upon a bald eagle's nest high in the top of a white pine on an

Canoe beached at the portage from Agamok Lake to Mueller Lake

Blueberries and reindeer moss

White cedars

Saganaga Lake

island on Lac La Croix. The parent eagles were not home, but two young ones, as large as adults, were trying their best to pull that big pine up by the roots! Clinging to thick branches near the nest, pumping away, they were building strong muscles in their broad wings, readying themselves for flight. Late that fall they very likely would fly to the Mississippi River somewhere below Lake Pepin, where they would winter. After the DDT problem with soft eggshells, it is a beautiful thing to have successful hatchings again.

Paddling around the big curve on Maraboef Lake, Fran and I came upon a large bear swimming across the lake ahead of us. The bear was nearing shore, so I paddled harder to get as good a look as possible when it climbed up the bank. There seemed to be a different plan up in the bow. Fran was backpaddling with gusto. I being stronger, we weren't too far from the bear when it touched bottom, and it splashed out of the water in great bounds, ran to the nearest tree, and scrambled up into the crown, huffing and puffing.

One grand experience that all Boundary Waters paddlers share is the presence of loons. They sometimes will swim quite close if you sit quietly in front of your camp. If they come close enough, their large size (five-foot wingspan) and blood-red eyes make their visit a very special event. Seeing one land or take off further emphasizes their great size and weight. Loons must run on the surface of the water for a long distance to be airborne. If one flies over you, listen. It's wing sounds say *big* and *fast*.

But it's the call of the loon that really gets to you. Rich, full-throated, loud and pure, the song varies from the lonesome *a-ooooo-a* in the middle of the night to the wild, laughing cry which rings of pure joy during flights. Love duets and "everybody-join-in" songfests can happen anytime in early summer.

Fran and I witnessed a great loon show from our favorite campsite on Ester Lake early one morning. A whole chorus of loons came swimming by, yodeling up a storm, and that exuberant concert was doubled in echoes off the high cliff behind our camp. They swam past us several times, seemingly enjoying the instant playback of their wild song. Then, with ecstatic clamor, all eight of them ran and flapped down the lake until their big black webs no longer touched the water, then retracted them as airliners do to streamline their bodies for

flight. Climbing in slowly ascending circles, they swung back over us, and in a grand finale, two pairs dropped down in a long slanting dive and, with wings upraised, *touched wings* in flight.

Quite often I have paddled back to my camp by starlight, or even on cloudy nights, sort of feeling my way home. But on one of the nights I stayed late with friends, I paddled all the way home on top of, beneath, and surrounded by northern lights. The lake was glass calm, so the midnight world looked the same right side up or upside down. Dancing reds and greens and misty blues were the background for island silhouettes, and the islands were unfolded inkblots. Not only was the night paddle no challenge, it was a new experience and pure delight.

The crackling fire in the little wood stove kept me cozy, the cold March wind whooshing through the pines around the tiny cabin let me know what I was cozy *from,* and Frederick Manfred's *Conquering Horse* held me at a pitch of excitement enough to dispel cabin fever in anyone.

I'd been out on snowshoes all day along the edge of the Boundary Waters Canoe Area Wilderness, trying to capture on film and in notes some of the wild beauty of that great boreal forest.

Cozy isn't a strong enough word. With a can of hot stew under my belt, tired muscles relaxing, and feeling good about what I'd seen on the ground glass of my cameras that day, I was reveling.

Lifting my eyes from the book to savor a lump-in-the-throat Manfred passage, I gazed out a small square window of the cabin, saw the sharp spires of northern conifers silhouetted against the late twilight, then lowered my head to continue reading. I glanced at my watch.

Double take! Twilight at 10 P.M. in March in northern Minnesota?

I opened the door and immediately knew — northern lights, brilliant! I threw on a sweater, wool cap, and chopper mits and started out the door, got smart and reached back for my parka.

The trees around the cabin limited my view of the sky, but I could tell through the patchwork openings that the show above was outstanding. There was a cold, silver-blue, shadowless light that showed considerable detail even in the thick forest. Talking to myself and to the aurora ("Please don't fade!"), I scurried down the frozen snowshoe trail (if I slipped off I'd be thigh-deep in the soft snow) toward the lake, until I came to an opening in the trees.

Straight above me, with its head at the zenith, body and tail to the south, and great wings spreading beyond the trees both east and west, was a diaphanous silver thunderbird, flashing and pulsating, then changing while I watched and exclaimed (with no one to hear) into a great eagle half as big as the sky itself. And then, just as quickly, the figure became a gauzy luna moth.

The amazing thing was that outside the phosphorescent figures the sky was as rich a black, and the stars were just as brilliant, as on any clear north-woods moonless night. The aurora was its brightest on the outlines of the figures, giving them startling clarity. The great pines, spruces, and firs around the clearing were clearly recognizable in sharp silhouette against the bright forms — *white* pines, *white* spruces, *balsam* firs.

As nice as this setting was, I didn't know what I might be missing behind the surrounding trees, so during a lull in the zenith display, I hurried down the path to the lake and out to the auger hole that was my source of water. From there I could see the flashing sky to far horizons in all directions except behind the cabin point.

To the north, classic transparent curtains flared and faded in graceful folds, their undulating bottom edges visible through the filmy wisps in broad, sweeping curves, like old-fashioned Christmas candy. In all other directions, searchlight beams flashed from horizon to zenith, forming a huge dome of dancing light. Straight above, where the thunderbird, eagle, and moth had been, bright ribbons of light were still tying themselves in twisting knots, forming and re-forming bright, curving, baroque frames around velvet-black, diamond-studded pieces of night.

The intensity of the display almost made me expect some sort of sound with it — crackling, snapping, singing, thunder, tympani, symphony — something. Were it portrayed in a movie, there *would* have been some grand accompaniment. Perhaps, though, down there alone on the wild lake, the cold northwest wind whistling around my parka hood was more fitting.

Basswood Falls, Minnesota-Ontario border

*This whisky-jack (gray jay) and its mate kept me
company on a solo on Daniels Lake. — C. B.*

River otter

Red pines

March thaw, Seagull River

HARDWOODS AND HILLS

Craig

Far beneath a tracery of bare branches, among ancient trunks of maple, basswood, elm, and oak, from under the winter-bleached carpet of fallen leaves, the beginnings of a new growing season are quietly proclaimed by tiny pink, white, and lavender blossoms.

It is a fine time to be in the hardwoods. I appreciate the texture of the untrodden spring soil — spongy with moisture, rich with another year's addition to the humus.

Even before the snow disappears from shaded hollows, sun-warmed south slopes give off the nutty aroma of topsoil. It is the smell of life, a prelude to fragrances sweeter.

Each year a black ash swamp near our home swells with run-off. An intermittent stream flows from it into a beaver pond after tumbling downhill for about two hundred yards. In late April bright clumps of round-lobed hepatica bloom high on its banks. Wild leeks push up in moist depressions — green swordsmen leading the progression of wild ginger, early meadow rue, and dwarf ginseng.

The ash swamp fills with marsh marigolds, then marsh blue violets and tall, elegant blue flags.

A little rise at the edge of the swamp boasts a covering of creamy wild oats; its relative, the large-flowered bellwort, grows just down the slope.

The banks of the brook host a succession of woodland wildflowers, with the showiest coming in early June. Like butterflies emerging from translucent chrysalises, yellow lady's slippers open spiraled wings, revealing waxy golden bodies.

Our woods near Moose Lake is at the north end of the hardwoods and the southern extent of the boreal forest. Once tall white pines crowned the mixed forest, but selective logging has removed most of these giants from the skyline. Rusted enameled buckets and early logging equipment still lie in the woods, left from the time our land was cut over in the 1940s.

To the south, the hardwoods are the predominant trees. Once a vast deciduous forest covered most of the area from north central Minnesota to the southeastern corner of the state. Part of this forest became known as The Big Woods. It grew on the fertile soil of a moraine that stretches from near St. Cloud southeast to Faribault.

This moraine and the rest of the rolling hills of central Minnesota are glacial deposits that were left in mounds as the ice sheets stuttered in their advances and retreats.

For most Minnesotans these are the woods and hills of home — the forests that border our farms,

93

Jack-in-the-pulpit

Wild ginger

Marsh marigolds

where youngsters stalk gray squirrels and cottontails with single-shot .22s, the woodlots that fuel our fireplaces and wood stoves. They are the oaks, maples, and elms in which we built tree houses, where we took sleigh rides, and that in recent years we invaded with suburban residences.

Unlike the more fragile habitats of prairie and northern forests, the deciduous woodlands have a resiliency both in plants and in animals. If man's encroachment into the hardwoods is not too severe, it is often forgiven, and in some cases even benefits some animals.

Man-made openings, such as fields and pastures or small logging operations, all create diversity within the forest habitat. The edges of woods bordering these openings have an abundance of undergrowth that provides cover and food for wildlife. Deer and other animals supplement their natural diets with corn and alfalfa. Foxes, hawks, and owls patrol fields for small rodents. If the openings are abandoned, the deciduous woodlands will reclaim the land within a few decades.

However resilient the hardwoods may be, much of this ecosystem has been lost due to the wide-scale clearing of The Big Woods for agricultural use. Only remnant virgin stands still exist, such as Nerstrand Woods in the state park south of Northfield.

Minnesota has a harsh climate, a short growing season. Plants of the deciduous forest have only about four months in which they must grow new foliage, flower, and ripen their seeds. By midsummer only a few species are still in blossom in the densely shaded woods. Acres of trilliums have long since blushed pink and withered. Dutchman's-breeches and other flowers that blossomed in the spring sunshine have been lost among the growth of Pennsylvania sedge and maple seedlings that now cover the forest floor. For most of the wildflowers this is a time of ripening. Rose twisted-stalk, clintonia, jack-in-the-pulpit, baneberry, and others hang heavy with swelling fruits — bright beads strung on shining green threads.

As the days shorten and the nights begin to freeze, chlorophyll fades from the leaves of trees and shrubs, revealing yellow pigments. If it has been a sunny fall, sugars manufactured in some leaves turn them a bright red.

Just as the wildflowers bloomed at various times throughout the spring, the leaves of different trees have their own timetables for turning color and dropping in the fall. The ash and walnuts shed their leaves weeks before the last of the oaks have turned. The woods become a tapestry of rich ambers, golds, reds, and greens. Acorns pop underfoot. A glowing light fills the woods as leaves drift down from the canopy, once again letting sunlight into the forest.

After the splash of fall color and the warm quiet days of Indian summer, the first really cold nights crystallize small ponds, encasing fallen leaves beneath the ice.

For two seasons I have gone into our woods at this time of year in pursuit of venison. Like many of Minnesota's deer hunters, I have looked forward not only to providing my family with meat, but to getting away from work and into the forest. For me the distance traveled was not far — a quarter-mile hike the first year and a half-mile this year to a platform of boards nailed to a clump of three maple trunks.

The spot I chose this year was situated at the junction of three heavily used deer trails where they cross a stream between alder swamps. The woods had a ridge of red maple, with an understory of mountain maple the deer had been browsing, and swales of black ash and aspen.

I ate a hearty breakfast opening morning and was on my stand before sunup. A gray squirrel was the first animal to show up. It bounded from the base of one tree to another, found an acorn, quickly dug a little hole, put the acorn in, and tamped the leaves back over it. A pair of chickadees came flitting about from the snow-dusted, leafy ground to the trunks of trees, investigating every hiding place that might produce a tidbit of food. One landed on a trunk about two inches from my face, peeked at me, and was off again.

Around midmorning a group of does walked by into the alders north of me. Moments later another doe came crashing through the brush and stopped only a few yards away. She saw me, snorted, and leaped off.

A red-backed vole was scurrying about beneath my stand when another movement caught my eye. A young buck came slowly walking across the stream. His antlers were a dark burnished bronze, deeply furrowed, with a small first tine and a broad blade that split at the end.

I had hoped for a larger deer, so I didn't raise my rifle. He was on a trail that would take him within twenty feet of my stand. The breeze was from him to me, but I was sure he'd get wind of me as he passed below.

About thirty feet from me he stopped and

Large-flowered trilliums

Yellow lady's slipper

Red fox

Bur oak, mixed hardwoods, Bloomington

Rose twisted-stalk

Northern hardwoods, Moose Lake

looked up, straight into my eyes. I didn't blink. For a solid ten seconds we stared at each other, then he bit off a twig, looked back up at me to make sure I hadn't moved, then proceeded right under me without taking another look or picking up my scent.

I dropped my buck with a single shot two mornings later. The day was clear and warming, quickly melting the light covering of snow.

After field dressing the deer, I pulled it a little way and paused to rest beneath a white pine. Four ravens were already at the viscera, performing their scavenger duties with apparent relish.

From one life to the next, the ways of nature almost defy the term *death*. There is only a transfer of energy as it is passed along in closely balanced cycles.

Winter Solstice 1982

I awoke this morning at a friend's home overlooking a small wild-shored lake in Edina. The first light came soft and gray, revealing a winter landscape of thick-boled oaks cloaked in fluttering leaves. The oaks were growing on a hill that rose steeply from the lake, blocking the rising sun until almost nine o'clock. We rejoiced at seeing the sunbeams finally clear the crest — the longest night of the year put behind us.

When I was growing up near here in the 1960s, this was the edge of the suburbs. Beyond here the hills that overlooked small farms were nearly all wooded and wild. They had a sense of permanence to them. At least to the eyes of a young boy, the city was city and the country was country and always would be.

Yet within about ten years the line dividing these two areas dissolved, and the freeways and suburbs flowed out over the hillsides. I remember being devastated watching a hill I liked to climb mined of its gravel until it was gone and warehouses placed as monuments to its memory. Neighboring fields and woods became housing developments and shopping centers.

Fortunately, about the same time, planners realized the value of open spaces within our cities and residential areas. City nature centers and county parks have been set aside, preserving at least a part of this land of lakes, marshes, rolling woodlands, and remnant prairies.

I'm afraid I will never be able to return to my childhood haunts without feeling a tremendous loss, but for the people who never knew the land before recent developments, the area will amaze them with its abundance of parks, wildlife, and green spaces.

The year's first ice on a woodland pond

Buck and doe white-tailed deer

THE DRIFTLESS AREA

Craig

Morning sun backlights the rippled surface of a sand dune, a high ridge in the distance blends with the sky — blue and hazy. A pair of falcons rip through the air, giving chase to a dove as they skim over a prairie. Trout dart under rafts of watercress in a cool stream. A bald eagle surveys its realm from a gnarled juniper on a limestone ledge. A wide river turns white with migrating whistling swans.

Images of the West? Read on . . . A hardwood forest includes Kentucky coffee trees, black oaks, shagbark hickories, butternuts, and black walnuts. A strutting wild turkey shows off his iridescent feathers to a demure hen. Maidenhair ferns open their circular fronds in moist hollows.

Appalachians? No, this is the Driftless Area of southeastern Minnesota, a unique land that escaped the last glaciers and thus was not buried by the glacial drift that covers most of the state in the form of rolling, lake-strewn terrain. In fact, this area has a drainage system so advanced in age that there are few if any lakes within it.

Even though the area was not covered by the last glaciation, glacial meltwater had a profound effect on the region by carving the magnificent valley that now holds the Mississippi River and the many smaller valleys of its tributaries.

The majority of the meltwater came via the predecessor of the Minnesota River, Glacial River Warren, which drained Glacial Lake Agassiz. The River Warren emptied into the Mississippi through the broad valley now crossed by the Mendota Bridge at Fort Snelling and was joined just downstream by the St. Croix, which was swollen with water from Glacial Lake Duluth. Together the three rivers created a tremendous eroding torrent that cut a valley miles wide and in some places eight hundred feet deep.

When I try to imagine what this river must have been like, I think of the glacial-fed rivers I have seen in the far north. Boiling and churning, silver-gray with their loads of abrasive particles, the rivers cut at the banks, causing great slabs of earth to tumble into the waters and be carried away.

As the flow in the Mississippi diminished, it could no longer carry the sand and gravel the fast-moving tributaries dumped into it.

The present floodplain of the Mississippi is about two hundred feet above the original valley floor, flowing over this sediment. One of the tributaries, the Chippewa River, entering from Wisconsin, deposited so much sediment that it impounded the Mississippi River and formed the twenty-two-mile-long Lake Pepin.

Kellogg-Weaver Dunes

Mississippi River from O. L. Kipp State Park

Sugar maples

Queen's Bluff, O. L. Kipp State Park

Whitewater Wildlife Area

Whitewater River, Whitewater State Park

Sugar maple

Sharp-lobed hepatica

From Lake Pepin south for three hundred miles, the entire floodplain has been designated as the Upper Mississippi River Wildlife and Fish Refuge. Its quiet backwaters, shallow bays of arrowhead and lotus, floodplain forests of cottonwood and willows, and hundreds of islands create one of the finest wildlife areas anywhere.

In the spring and fall, the riverway is one of the nation's main thoroughfares for migrating waterfowl. It is the major wintering ground for bald eagles of the north central United States, and it is the permanent home of beavers, muskrats, mink, river otters, raccoons, and many other kinds of water-related species, including a large variety of fish.

I am drawn to the Mississippi not only by its impressive wilderness habitats, but because it has been a corridor for man's travels into Minnesota since the earliest explorers.

Its history and lore intrigue me, and its hazy, endless pathway beckons my adventurous spirit to follow its course, drifting with ghosts of keelboats and steamers through the watery wilderness from one river town to the next.

This was the route followed by some of Minnesota's first settlers, and it was to fuel the steamboats' boilers that many of the riverbank trees were felled.

One of the logging operations was at what is now Latch State Park. From atop the three bluffs at Latch — Faith, Hope, and Charity — the river is seen about 450 feet below. Today tugs push barges up and down the river, and the trees have grown back on the slopes. The era of the old steamboats passed without much of a trace. Yet when the river is covered with fog and the whole valley is silent, visions of paddle-wheelers do not seem so far distant. In fact, a few replicas of the old paddle-wheelers again stir the waters, carrying tourists on a nostalgic journey into the past.

The spectacular bluffs above Highway 61 are covered with an incredible variety of vegetation. Prairies grow on southwest slopes, while the north and east sides support hardwood forests. Near the base of the bluffs, black walnuts and white pines flourish. Red cedars and junipers grow on some bluffs, and on Queen's Bluff there is a relict stand of white cedar.

At Kipp State Park, trails leading to promontories with panoramic views of the river wind through stands of shagbark hickory, one of the many trees growing there that are at the northern extent of their range.

The stream-dissected land inland from the Mississippi has been eroded by four main tributaries, the Root, Zumbro, Cannon, and Whitewater rivers. Each of these rivers and their classic branching tributary systems carried glacial run-off from the west. The landscape they created looks more like the foothills and valleys of the Black Hills of South Dakota than what most people think of as Minnesota.

It was in these broad valleys, probably in the 1840s, that some of the first farms in southeastern Minnesota were established. A treaty with the Sioux in 1851 opened the land to legal settlement by whites. First wheat and then other crops and livestock were brought in. Soon, however, the farmers lost the battle with nature. Denuded by clearing and grazing, large parts of the steep-walled valleys were washed away in flash floods. Farms were covered with mud and debris. The hills were left gullied, the streams muddy, and the farmers moved on.

Today, almost the whole of the Driftless Area lies within the boundaries of the Richard J. Dorer Memorial Hardwood State Forest. Dorer recognized the damage farming had done to this land and its potential to once again become a fine wildlife area.

During the 1950s, Dorer served as the state Supervisor of the Bureau of Game. Under his direction, work was begun primarily in the Whitewater River valley, planting hillsides and blocking gullies. Proper farming practices were established, grazing was eliminated where it damaged the terrain, and a plan to place the land under state ownership and protection was begun. Dorer's and other like-minded conservationists' work paid off. The hills and valleys of southeastern Minnesota have stabilized and today support our most diverse hardwood forests.

Two weeks after the peak of fall color along the North Shore of Lake Superior, I was camped at Whitewater State Park east of Rochester. By that time the fall color had moved south, and the hillsides were turning the rich antique reds of oaks accented by golden aspens. I hiked a wide circle, climbing up to limestone outcrops with views over the valley, and back down switchback trails.

I flushed ruffed grouse, sneaked up to a stream edge and watched trout in the clear water, then hiked back up to the rim again. Red-tailed hawks were circling overhead, garter snakes were sunning themselves on grassy outcrops. Unlike on the North Shore, where sightseers fill every motel and

Mixed hardwoods, Beaver Creek Valley State Park

camp site during the color peak, I was alone. I had seen one young couple as I started out, and hiked all day on the marked trails without encountering another person. The Driftless Area might better have been named the Forgotten Land.

Even in midsummer I have felt I had parts of these southern hardwoods all to myself. At Beaver Creek Valley State Park, the steep slopes covered with ferns, wildflowers, and towering trees held me captive for days of tranquil wandering.

In August I found the sharp-lobed hepatica leaves with a patina of satiny maroon. In May I had seen them at Frontenac, filled with blossoms, their bright greeting to spring witnessed by few people.

Why, I wonder, has this land been so undiscovered by tourists? Are we so addicted to lakes we cannot explore a land that has none? To be sure, many of us have driven along the Mississippi, awed by the mountainlike lines of bluffs, subdued by the tranquillity of the slow-moving river. We drive down to see the apple blossoms, and later to collect the sweet fruits of autumn. A few cast lines into the trout streams, hunt ducks in the backwaters, canoe the Root or spend a weekend camping at Whitewater. But the land has more to offer than we can absorb in just a few days.

It is a landscape geologically out of step with the rest of the state; it wears the face of time. Perhaps it is this sense of time it offers most, and maybe because it takes time to perceive this, few of us have come to appreciate the Driftless Area. For those of us who have, it remains a land rich in diversity, with room enough for a lifetime of uncrowded discovering.

PRAIRIE PASSAGES

Craig

Minnesota grasslands are mostly tall grass prairies, yet within these there exists a vast array of differing habitats. The tall grasses — big bluestem, or turkeyfoot, named after its "three-toed" seed heads, Indian grass, and switch grass — are the sod-forming grasses of the eastern prairies. Mixed in with these on drier grounds are the bunchgrasses — needlegrass, little bluestem, side oats grama, June grass, and Canadian rye.

The grasses are the binders of the prairie; the nutritious fodder of bison, pronghorn, and in recent times, cattle and sheep; the nesting cover and food for waterfowl and upland game birds. But the jewels of the prairies are the forbs, the flowering broadleaf plants that bloom in succession through the summer and autumn months.

I grew up in what was then Eden Prairie Township on the outer edge of the Twin Cities. The land was largely wild — rolling wooded moraines and marshy-shored lakes. Tucked in here and there were truck farms that produced strawberries, raspberries, and a wide assortment of vegetables.

Back then I knew little about prairies other than they were what we crossed on the way to the mountain west. Eden Prairie certainly didn't look like that land, so why wasn't it named Eden Knolls or something more appropriate?

Well, there *had* been prairies in Eden Prairie, and there still are remnants if you know where to look. Once over a third of Minnesota was covered by native grasslands, but almost all were converted into farms (such as many of the truck farms in Eden Prairie) or covered by housing developments. Farther west they were either grazed or plowed under for croplands.

It wasn't until the 1970s that many Minnesotans began discovering the splendors that our forebears found when they arrived at the prairies.

I was introduced to grassland habitats at the Hennepin County park reserves. At Richardson Nature Center, I was shown the ingenious way the needlegrass seeds have evolved to plant themselves, using a long awn (the threadlike part attached to the seed) that twists corkscrewlike with moisture and drying to drill the seed into the ground.

A group of us searched through the grasses at Richardson and found drab-leaved leadplants, columns of blazing-star flowers, and asters of many sizes and colors. The cross-pollinators — butterflies, bees, and other insects — were everywhere.

Monarch butterfly on blazing star

Black-eyed Susans

Asters and goldenrod — late-blooming forbs at Richardson Nature Center

When the pioneers first came to farm Minnesota, they saw few trees growing on the prairie, and some felt the grasslands must not be as fertile as the woods. They were wrong. The land had deep, rich soil that would one day be among the most productive in the nation. But in one respect they were right: prairies exist only because most trees cannot survive there. There are two major factors that limit tree growth on the prairie, neither of them having to do with soil fertility. The first is moisture. The western parts of Minnesota, which were predominantly prairie, receive too little rainfall to support most trees. The second factor is fire. Prairie plants are well adapted to periodic burning, but fires kill most young trees; thus even areas with sufficient moisture to support trees will stay prairie as long as they are burned every few years.

It is possible that many of Minnesota's prairies were extended eastward by Native Americans periodically burning the grasslands. They may have set fires for many reasons — to create green pastures that would attract the grazing and browsing animals such as elk, deer, bison, and pronghorn, and as a tool in hunting them; to rid the land of insects and disease; and to clear the woods of underbush, making travel and hunting easier and sneak attacks from enemies less likely. For whatever reasons, man-set fires probably occurred frequently, steadily killing back the deciduous forest edge, allowing the prairie to advance eastward.

The prairie at Richardson Nature Center is typical of many prairie areas that once existed among the hills of the Twin Cities. The grasses and forbs were dependent on fire to keep the surrounding woods from invading them. Bur oak, a tree that has evolved to be fire resistant, especially after it is a few years old, forms the first line of trees at the edge of the grasses and occasionally grows right out in the open prairie.

In southeastern Minnesota, the south- and southwest-facing bluffs are covered by "goat prairies," extremely steep grasslands where it was said only goats could graze. Besides being the hottest, driest slopes in summer, these hillsides soak up the winter sun, thawing many days during the winter. This thawing and refreezing chokes the roots of nonprairie plants, keeping the grasslands open.

Near the town of Weaver in the Mississippi River valley, another type of prairie exists. This land of oak savanna and shifting sand dunes has many plants especially adapted to surviving on a transient landscape.

The proper management of Minnesota's remaining prairies is now being studied. At Big Stone National Wildlife Refuge, I observed a spring burn where refuge workers have replaced Native Americans in the role of fire starters.

I met with the refuge staff on the rolling prairie bluffs overlooking the Minnesota River. Below us the bottomlands were alive with fresh new growth, but where we stood, life had been stifled by a thick mat of dead grasses that had built up over many years.

As the sun rose higher, a warm breeze swept over the bluffs in the direction the refuge workers wished the fire to go. Just in case the wind switched, water trucks with crews were standing by.

Holding lighted torches down to the ground, the men walked over the slopes, leaving a trail of flames in the tinder-dry grass.

The wind caught the flames, pulling the fire along in gusts. Black smoke mounted up like a billowing storm cloud. The sun became a garnet, day turned dark as dusk, and all the warm hues within the flames shown brilliantly.

Behind the fire line, white smoke spewed out from the ashes like miniature geysers.

The flames made their way over the bluffs down to the river bottoms, flashed across cattails, and sizzled at the water's edge.

A dead cottonwood caught fire, its hollow trunk drawing flames up like a chimney.

As I watched, mesmerized by the fire, the smoke, and the changed look of the land, a red cedar exploded into a tower of orange streamers and thick black smoke. Whirlwinds of flame leaped into the air, and the fire skipped along faster and faster until reaching a green woods, where it quietly burned itself out.

Within a few weeks the burned area became the lushest stretch of the prairie. Bunchgrasses sent up fresh spears, and throughout the summer, flowers not seen there for many years bloomed.

To transform a stunted field back into a multicolored garden simply with the touch of a match seems a bit like magic. But restoring a damaged prairie is not always easy. Some areas of parks and refuges have been so degraded by past overgrazing or farming that the only way to regain the prairie habitat is to plow the weeds under and replant native grasses and flowers. Unfortunately, only a handful of the dozens of species can be

Granite outcrop at Big Stone National Wildlife Refuge — among the oldest rocks on the face of the earth

Ball cactus

Sharp-tailed grouse

seeded. It will take many years, if ever, for the rest of the plant life to fill in.

In the northwest corner of Minnesota, work is being done to help the birds that symbolize the native grasslands — the prairie chicken and its close relative the sharp-tailed grouse. Dad and I visited one of the study areas in the aspen parkland east of the Red River, where we witnessed some very special events of the prairie spring.

We were up ahead of the alarm set to go off at 3:00 A.M. We pulled on layers of wools, heavy outer clothing, and insulated boots — the mid-April nights were still freezing and we would be sitting for hours.

After a short drive, we turned onto a pull-off just past a ditch used as a landmark and got out into the night. A half-mile hike to the south brought us to a small canvas blind in the middle of an open prairie — the site of an ancestral dancing ground of the sharp-tailed grouse.

Tipping up one end of the blind, we set our equipment inside and lowered the blind over us. We pointed our tripod-mounted cameras out the small openings and settled into our chairs, listening to the prairie waking up.

Snipes circling overhead filled the air with repeated series of breathy, whistlelike notes created by wind vibrating through their fanned tail feathers. Then the first cooing of the sharptails began. We sat in silence, entranced by the primeval music as more and more species joined in.

Each of our state's ecosystems has its own unique sounds that mean *wildness*. On the prairie this wildness was sung in a chorus of many voices — frogs and snipes, greater prairie chickens and sharp-tailed grouse, the rattle of sandhill cranes and the honking of migrating geese. Each call had a specialness all its own, but together they became one voice, that of the prairie morning.

Our eyes searched the darkness outside the blind for the sources of the cooing and cackling, but for many minutes we couldn't locate the grouse. Then without having seen them arrive we were suddenly surrounded by sharptails.

From a leap into the air a male lit right in front of me. *Coo-o-oo!* The bright purplish neck sacs filled with air as he called. His yellow eye combs were fully raised and his tail stood straight up. He went into a foot-stamping, quill-rattling dance that at close range sounded like a jack hammer. *P'd'd'd'd'd'd'!* *P'd'd'd'd'd'd*! He turned and taxied over the ground. *P'd'd'd'd'd'd!* *P'd'd'd'd'd*! Broadside to

me he froze. Still posturing with sacs inflated, he held the stance for perhaps half a minute, then jumped into the air and repeated his dance a few feet away.

Each cock had a territory he defended by running up to the border and facing off against his neighbors. Most confrontations were nothing more than cackling matches with heads held low and wings spread, but occasionally the birds leaped at each other and feathers would fly.

The hens, which had been wandering among the displaying males, began to accept their choices of mates for the day. After copulating, the hens left and the cocks remained to display for any females still present. As with all grouse, both cocks and hens mate with a number of partners during the spring.

For a few minutes I watched a rough-legged hawk flying around to the west of us, then he headed our way. Between us and the approaching hawk a jackrabbit stood up and looked at the hawk. I expected the rabbit to dash away as the hawk swooped down at it, but instead he simply stood tall. The hawk pulled up and passed by; the rabbit hopped a few feet and started eating. The ability of the prey to know it was too big for the predator impressed me, but this ability would be demonstrated in even finer detail the next day.

Satisfied we had our photographs of the sharptails, we moved the blind about a mile to the southwest to a prairie chicken booming ground. Our walk to the blind the following morning was guided by a star we picked out by compass as we left the car. The blind was on an island in a marsh. Somewhere a dry ridge led out to it, but in the dark we both ended up splashing through six inches of water. One thing about rubber-bottomed boots, once the water's in, it isn't going to drain out. We spent the morning with soggy, cold feet.

Like the sharptails the morning before, the chickens appeared out of the darkness and began their booming almost as soon as we were in the blind.

The predawn light revealed the birds had territories not only on the islands in the marsh but also out in the tufts of grass lying above the water. The battling birds, often up to their bellies in water, sent it spraying into the air.

The prairie chickens, or pinnated grouse, as they are called for the pinnae feathers the males raise over their heads when displaying, do not have a loud foot-stomping show like the sharptails. Instead, their large orange neck sacs produce a much more resonant booming vocalization that carries over great distances. At the height of the activity the air was vibrating with a constant humming interspersed with the whoops that males make when a female is in the area and the gull-like laughs and cackles of showdowns and fights.

Suddenly there was a hush, and the birds crouched down in the grasses. A brown blur passed by the blind, and the ground erupted with flushing prairie chickens. The blur had been a female marsh hawk. She made a half-hearted attempt at pursuing one of the birds, then swung off to the east.

A number of male marsh hawks, which are gray rather than brown, had passed over before without causing the slightest alarm, but the female is larger and capable of taking a prairie chicken. The chickens are able to tell the difference and have learned they need only fear the females.

We spent an afternoon in the blind at this same location. The evening booming was not as exuberant as that of the morning, but we had a good show put on by short-eared owls. These prairie owls are superb fliers, with a characteristic fast upbeat and slow downbeat of their wings. Pairs of them put on tumbling air shows, chasing each other from one end of the prairie opening to the other. Many times they free fell, with wings fluttering above them until regaining control just above the ground, then flew almost straight up and repeated the aerobatics a few seconds later.

A cow moose sauntered out from an aspen island a quarter mile to the south of us. She browsed a bit, then curious about the blind, headed our way. When she was about a hundred yards away, she skirted around us until she got our scent and trotted to the cover of another pocket of aspens. At best, a cow moose is never going to win a beauty contest, but this one had half shed her winter coat. Her forequarters were nearly naked, accentuating her skinny neck and bulbous nose, and patches of dull hair were draped over the rest of her. We agreed she was the sorriest looking critter either of us had ever seen.

The prairie chickens flew off just before sunset, and we left the blind. On our way back to camp, we watched an owl land in a snag silhouetted against the still-glowing western sky.

It's ironic and sad that the once vast, unbroken prairie is now nearly gone. Our plows have cut the fibrous roots that bound the prairie, keeping it whole. Our cattle and sheep have overgrazed the native grasses and transported foreign weeds to the disturbed ground in their manure. The loss of habitat has in turn taken its toll on wildlife.

Having come to the important realization that prairie is worth saving, we are starting to reverse the process of its decimation.

Burning and seeding programs in wildlife refuges, state and county parks, and Nature Conservancy holdings are reestablishing native prairie habitats. Remnants will be saved. Pockets of vegetation will keep the essential gene pools alive, just as zoos propagate species extinct in the wild. But gone forever is the chance to roam across borderless expanses of wild prairie, where the night horizons are dark and grouse are flushed in flocks of hundreds instead of dozens.

We have destroyed the work of time and discovered we cannot restore life nearly as easily as we can take it away.

Prairie fire

Prairie chicken booming

Large-flowered beardtongue, bur oak

PHOTOGRAPHIC DATA

Most of the photographs were taken specifically for this book from 1980 through 1982. The earliest picture in the book was taken in 1962, and a few are from 1967 and 1968.

The majority of the photographs were taken with large-format view cameras: a Calumet 4 × 5, and a Wista M 450 that was adapted to a 5 × 7 format for several pictures. These cameras were fitted with Schneider lenses of the following focal lengths: 90mm, 120mm, 135mm, 150mm, 210mm, 240mm, and 300mm.

The cameras were mounted on heavy wooden tripods; Les used a Camera Equipment Company Professional Jr. movie tripod, and Craig a Zone VI tripod with a Bogen #3047 head.

The 4 × 5 inch and 5 × 7 inch film used was Ektachrome, with an ASA of 50 in the early pictures and 64 in the recent ones. This film was processed by Linhoff Color Photo Laboratories.

Where getting close to the subject, motion, or depth of field was a problem, 35mm Nikkormat cameras were used with the following Nikor lenses: 28mm, 55mm macro, 135mm, and 300mm.

Les mounted his 35mm on the Pro Jr. tripod, Craig used a Bogen #3020 tripod with a Bogen #3028 head for all of his 35mms except those taken from a floating blind, where the camera was braced on a crossbar. Kodachrome 64 was used for all of the 35mm work and was processed by Kodak.

Exposures were figured using a Sekonic incident light meter and the through-the-lens meters in the 35mm Nikkormats. Often both metering systems were used to figure a single exposure.

Photography Credits

Les — Pages 6, 9, 13, 21, 23, 32, 34, 37, 40 bottom, 45, 49, 50, 51, 53, 54, 55, 56, 57, 59, 60–61, 62, 64, 65, 70, 71, 73, 75, 76, 78, 90 bottom, 91, 92, 97, 102, 107 112, 122 bottom

Les and Craig — Pages 16, 107

Nadine Blacklock — Page 80

Craig — Pages 10, 15, 17, 18–19, 20, 25, 27, 28, 29, 31, 33, 35, 40 top, 41, 43, 52, 58, 63, 69, 72, 77, 79, 81, 83, 84, 85, 86, 89, 90 top, 94, 95, 98, 99, 100–101, 103, 105, 106, 109, 110–111, 113, 114, 115, 116, 117, 119, 122 top, 123, 125, 126, 127, 130, 131, 132